"The third edition of Brendan Kehoe's classic is still the best around. . . . it's worth every dime, especially if you're new to the Net."
— *Internet World,* January 1995

"Kehoe's style is light, engaging, and just right for the Net." —Jael Li-Ron, *PC/Computing*

"Kehoe really knows his stuff!"
—John Quittner, *Newsday*

"It's the best introductory guide to the Internet available." —Andrew Kantor, *PC Magazine*

"excellent book" —*Houston Chronicle*

"This Brendan Kehoe classic is still at the top of the stack."
—James W. Crawley, *San Diego Union-Tribune*

"A handy guide to have on one's bookshelf."
—Robyn Peters, *Media & Methods*

"It remains the best small book for the true beginner." —Peter Salus in ;login:

"Zen and the Art of the Internet is a wonderful paperback guide to those who are just starting to explore the Internet and are familiar with basic networking operations." —Computer User

"This new edition offers one thing the others have yet to offer: true enlightenment."
—Steve Brock

"Zen's solo author, Brendan Kehoe, brings humor, rhythm, and style to the work."
—Phil Hatch, *Network News* newsletter

"A classic introduction to the Internet."
—*The Wilson Quarterly*

"Written for the beginner, it provides a relatively painless entry to a very complex resource."
—Alexander W. Burawa in *MicroComputer Journal*

"It's still my favorite take-you-by-the-hand guide to what the Net is like from the outside."
—Elizabeth P. Crowe, *Computer Currents*

Zen
and the
Art of the
Internet

*A Beginner's
Guide*

Prentice Hall Series in Innovative Technology

Dennis R. Allison, David J. Farber, and Bruce D. Shriver   *Series Advisors*

Zen
and the
Art of the
Internet

A Beginner's Guide

Fourth Edition

Brendan P. Kehoe

For book and bookstore information

http://www.prenhall.com

Prentice Hall PTR
Upper Saddle River, New Jersey 07458

Library of Congress Cataloging-in-Publication Data

Kehoe, Brendan P.
Zen and the art of the internet : a beginner's guide/ Brendan P. Kehoe. -- 4th ed.
    p.   cm. (Innovative technology series)
Includes bibliographical references and index.
ISBN 0-13-452914-6
1. Internet (Computer network)   I. Title.   II. Series.
TK5105.875.I51K44   1996   95-37456
004.6'7--dc20   CIP

Editorial/Production Supervision and Interior Design: Joanne Anzalone
Acquisitions Editor: Karen Gettman
Buyer: Alexis Heydt
Cover Design: Anthony Gemmellaro
Cover Design Direction: Jerry Votta
Art Director: Gail Cocker-Bogusz

 © 1996 Prentice Hall PTR

Prentice Hall, Inc.

A Paramount Communications Company

Upper Saddle River, NJ 07458

The publisher offers discounts on this book when ordered in bulk quantities.
For more information, contact:

Corporate Sales Department
PTR Prentice Hall
1 Lake Street
Upper Saddle River, NJ 07458
Phone: 800-382-3419
FAX: 201-236-7141
E-mail: corpsales@prenhall.com

Printed in the United States of America

10 9 8 7 6 5 4 3 2 1

ISBN 0-13-452914-6

Prentice-Hall International (UK) Limited, London
Prentice-Hall of Australia Pty. Limited, Sydney
Prentice-Hall of Canada, Inc., Toronto
Prentice-Hall Hispanoamericana S.A., Mexico
Prentice-Hall of India Private Limited, New Delhi
Prentice-Hall of Japan, Inc., Tokyo
Simon & Schuster Asia Pte. Ltd., Singapore
Editora Prentice-Hall do Brasil, Ltda., Rio de Janeiro

Dedicated to
Mary Ellen Miner
and
Frank Hackett

Thanks.

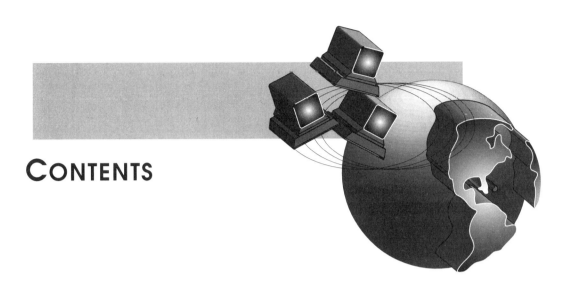

CONTENTS

4 Usenet News   *41*

8 Commercial Services 111

9 Things You'll Hear About 119

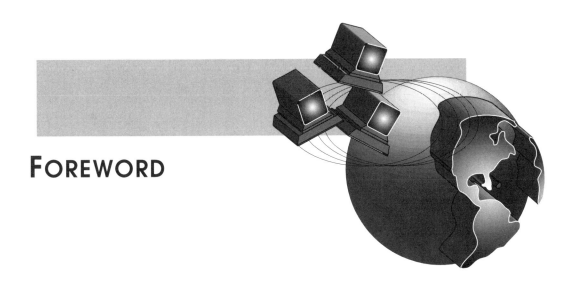

FOREWORD

One of the wonderful things about working on the Internet is the near guarantee that help will arrive from unexpected places. In this case, a local guide prepared so that a system administrator at a small college wouldn't have to answer so many pesky questions about how to use the Net has turned out to be just the key to helping people all over the world get up to speed on the way the Internet works.

Zen and the Art of the Internet is more than just a collection of recipes of how to connect to this or that site or what arcane commands to type at what prompts. There's a lot of that, to be sure—the Net still has what John Perry Barlow terms a "savage user interface," and some amount of hand-holding is needed to guide people through the rough spots. Much more than that, though, *Zen* gives the new user of the Net some clue as to *why* things are as they are, how people interact in this environment, and an approach to make their use of the Internet less of a hunt through the wilderness.

Brendan has written a book which has been on the wish lists of network builders for a long time—a clear, straightforward, and engaging description of what the Internet is and why you want to be connected to it. While large sums of money may build bigger and faster networks, *Zen* argues that it is the mass of well-trained, literate, and interesting people *behind* the wires and computers that makes them really successful.

Edward Vielmetti
Ann Arbor, MI
emv@tubed.com

"I think, though, that if I suddenly found myself in the, to me, unthinkable position of facing a class in English usage and style, I would simply lean far out over the desk, clutch my lapels, blink my eyes, and say, 'Get the little book! Get the little book! Get the little book!'"

—E.B. White,
introduction to Strunk and White's
The Elements of Style.

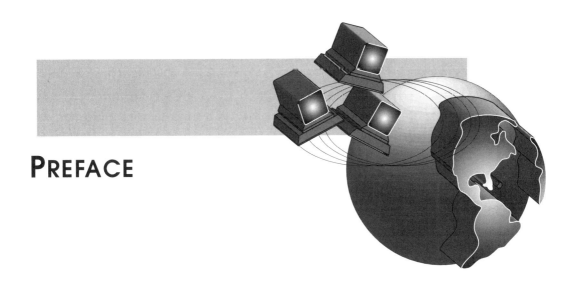

PREFACE

When historians travel through the records of a century, seeking those events that had a pronounced impact on society as a whole, they often find ideas that were originally nothing more than passing thoughts.

Over time, these inspirations grew to affect the daily life of millions of people. The car, the telephone, finding a cure for illnesses like the polio virus, all of these discoveries made a notable impression on the global culture.

What you are now pursuing—this global method of communications known as *networking*—will be seen to have had a similar effect. Look at our world today: friends staying in touch across the oceans; researchers sharing their results not in terms of days or weeks, but *minutes*; couples being married after having met in Cyberspace; and most of all, a generation being born to communicating with other nations as if it were a commonplace occurrence.

The uncountable millions of people all becoming

involved in this world-wide sharing of information each started out with the curiosity you're now feeling. You've heard the Internet mentioned on TV, in the newspaper, in cartoons, cvcn in cvcry-day conversations. So you've finally decided to "take the leap" and learn how to use this new medium—to see if it meets the grand predictions you've been told.

This book is intended to ease you into this new world. As you go along, you'll find new ways to talk, new ways to think. If you encounter areas of this virtual world that leave you confused or frustrated, don't give up. Odds are you know someone who can explain that particular area to you. And most of all, realize that it's like any other aspect of life: the potential routes are uncountable. Choose your pursuits carefully, and know that the Internet is used by a community driven by its desire to share information with others. It has grown from an interesting idea by some very influential and creative people, to become a veritable backbone to modern society.

Enjoy your travels.

brendan@zen.org

Mountain View, CA

*"Forward, forward let us range,
Let the great world spin for ever
down the ringing grooves of change."*
— Alfred, Lord Tennyson,
LocksleyHall, l. 181.

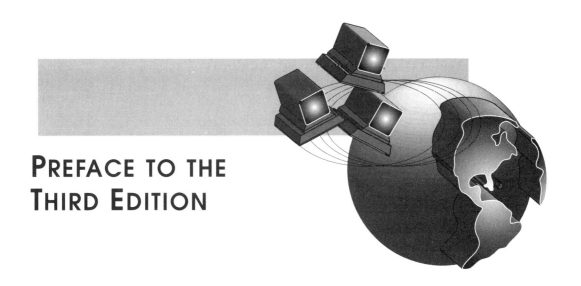

PREFACE TO THE THIRD EDITION

The Internet has come of age.

In the United States, the 1992 Presidential campaign had an unparalleled presence in Cyberspace. Candidates sported email addresses, electronically available position papers, and a heretofore unseen awareness of this "global village." In the former Soviet Union, email was one of the only ways citizens could get information out about the coup against then-President Gorbachev. And MTV is on the Net.

For those who helped build the Internet, its fantastic growth—more than doubling in size each six months—has been both exciting and sobering. Many predict that in only a few years, Internet connectivity will be available by right, in much the same way as having access to a telephone is considered a basic necessity.

To someone learning about the Net for the first time, the sheer size of it can be overwhelming. Many people feel a strong urge to panic when they first encounter the Internet, putting it on a list of things to avoid, like learning to program a VCR. I urge you to stick with it and set your own pace. You alone control your learning process. If you need to, learn to program your VCR first, so you can tape the shows you'll miss when you're traveling through Cyberspace. Then start reading, keeping in mind that in a day or two, you'll have learned enough to actually help others use the Net.

In 1968, just before the birth of what became the Internet, J.C.R. Licklider and Robert Taylor wrote about virtual communities; a quarter of a century later, their words perfectly describe what's happened on the Net.

> *What will on-line interactive communities be like? In most fields they will consist of geographically separated members, sometimes grouped in small clusters and sometimes working individually. They will be communities not of common location but of common interest.*

And thus begins the web.

brendan@zen.org
Santa Cruz, CA

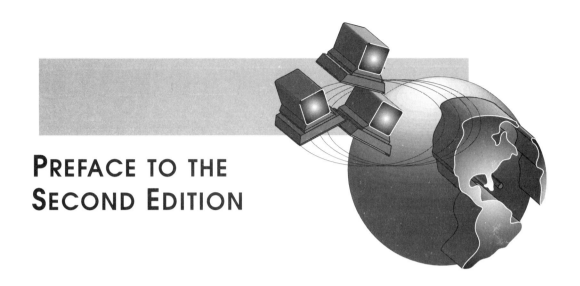

PREFACE TO THE SECOND EDITION

Welcome to Cyberspace!

We've been expecting you. Be careful as you try out your new legs—the ground's firm, but does have some unexpected twists and turns. This book will be your guide through a vast and amazing web of new people, places, and ideas.

Zen is intended for computing novices and experienced researchers alike. It attempts to remain operating-system "neutral"—little information herein is specific to DOS, Unix, VMS, or any other environment. In its early stages, this book prompted response from a vast and disparate audience—from librarians to hobbyists to carpenters to Ph.D. physicists. It's my hope that it will be useful to nearly anyone.

Some typographical conventions are maintained throughout. All abstract items like possible filenames, usernames, etc., are represented in *italics*. Similarly, definite filenames and email addresses are represented in a quoted 'typewriter' font. A user's session is usually offset from the rest of the paragraph, as such:

```
prompt> command
        The results are usually displayed here.
```

The purpose of this book is twofold: first, it will serve as a reference piece which you can easily grab on-the-fly to look something up. You'll also gain a foundation from which you can explore your surroundings at your leisure. *Zen and the Art of the Internet* doesn't spend a significant amount of time on any one point; rather, it provides enough for people to learn the specifics of what their local system offers.

One warning is perhaps in order—this territory we are entering can become a fantastic time-sink. Hours can slip by, people can come and go, and you'll be locked in Cyberspace. Remember to do your work!

With that, it's my distinct pleasure to usher you into the Net.

brendan@zen.org
Chester, PA

ACKNOWLEDGMENTS

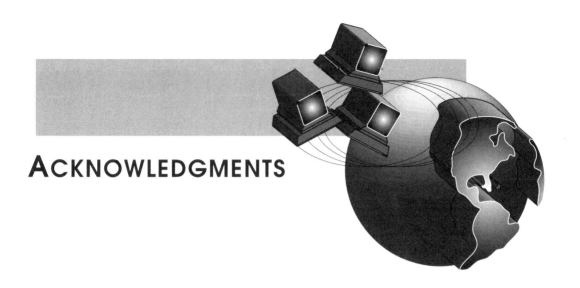

Certain sections in this booklet are not my original work—rather, they are derived from documents that were available on the Internet and already aptly stated their areas of concentration. The main section on Archie was derived from 'whatis.archie' by Peter Deutsch, then of the McGill University Computing Centre. It's available via anonymous FTP from archie.ans.net. Some of what's in the telnet section came from an impressive introductory document put together by SuraNet, along with a few discoveries from Scott Yanoff's list. Some definitions in the glossary are from an excellent one put together by Colorado State University.

It would be remiss of me not to thank those who provided the moral and inspirational support that has been so invaluable throughout this whole process: Sven Heinicke, at whose house I wrote a good 40 percent of the first edition of the guide over a Christmas break in college; Jennifer Kowaleuski Loughlin; Chip Page; and Patrick Quairoli, for his grace under pressure. My thanks to Jeffrey Osier, for all of his help, great music, and unending support, and to Mary Ellen Miner, for her wonderful friendship. I'm quite proud to call them my friends.

Zen would not be the same without the aid of many people on the Net, and the providers of resources that are already out there. Many, many people sent in encouraging notes and a few corrections for mistakes or changes in the second edition. I'd also like to thank the folks who provided much-needed information on-the-fly or gave comments, suggestions, and criticisms to early drafts of the guide and its parts: Andy Blankenbiller, Vint Cerf, Alan Emtage, Brian Fitzgerald, John Goetsch, Jeff Kellem, Bill Krauss, Steve Lodin, Mike Nesel, Bob Neveln, Wanda Pierce, Joshua Poulson, Dave Sill, Bob Smart, Gene Spafford, Ed Vielmetti, Craig Ward, and Chip Yamasaki. Glee Willis of the University of Nevada-Reno deserves particular mention for all of her work—this guide would have been considerably less polished without her help.

On New Year's Eve of 1993, I was involved in a nearly fatal car accident. According to statistics related to the severity of the injuries, I'm not even supposed to be able to have simple conversations, much less talk about the Internet. (Indeed, those statistics would suggest that I wasn't supposed to have lived through it.) Words cannot begin to express my gratitude to Dr. Elizabeth Sandel of the Hospital of the University of Pennsylvania. Her absolutely incredible (some have termed "miraculous") work is unparalleled.

The title of *Zen* is based on two others: The first, *Zen and the Art of Motorcycle Maintenance* by Robert Pirsig, is a fantastic work describing an approach to life that was taken in the design of this book. The second, *Zen in the Art of Archery* by Eugen Herrigel, is the true source of the application of "Zen" to the title. It is the true source of the whole series of books given similar titles.

As is often obligatory in an acknowledgments page, I'd like to thank the music of Seal, Garnet Rogers, Sarah McLachlan, Harry Connick, Jr., and Drew Youngs. Keeping their songs playing in the background while working on the book helped considerably.

Finally, mixed thanks to Anne Rice, whose books *The Witching Hour*, *Lasher*, and *Taltos* were absolutely fantastic. I got so hooked that I ended up just barely meeting my deadlines—twice.

"Think where man's glory most begins and ends
And say my glory was I had such friends."
— W.B. Yeats, "The Municipal Gallery Revisited"

1 NETWORK BASICS

We are truly in an information society. Now more than ever, moving vast amounts of information quickly across great distances is one of our most pressing needs. From small one-person entrepreneurial efforts to the largest of corporations, more and more professional people are discovering that the only way to be successful in the '90s and beyond is to realize that technology is advancing at a breakneck pace—and they must somehow keep up. Likewise, researchers from all corners of the earth are finding that their work thrives in a networked environment. Immediate access to the work of colleagues and a "virtual" library of millions of volumes and thousands of papers affords them the ability to incorporate a body of knowledge heretofore unthinkable. Work groups can now conduct interactive conferences with each other, paying no heed to physical location—the possibilities are endless.

You have at your fingertips the ability to talk in "real

time" with someone in Japan, send a 2,000-word short story to a group of people who will critique it for the sheer pleasure of doing so, see if a Macintosh sitting in a lab in Canada is turned on, and find out if someone happens to be sitting in front of their computer (*logged on*) in Australia, all inside of thirty minutes. No airline (or Tardis, for that matter) could ever match that travel itinerary.

The largest problem people face when first using a network is grasping all that's available. Even seasoned users find themselves surprised when they discover a new service or feature that they'd never known even existed. Once they are acquainted with the terminology and sufficiently comfortable with making occasional mistakes, their learning process will drastically speed up.

Domains

Getting where you want to go can often be one of the more difficult aspects of using networks. The variety of ways in which places are named will probably leave a blank stare on your face at first. Don't fret; there is a method to this apparent madness.

If you were to ask for a home address, you would probably expect a street, apartment, city, state, and zip code. That's all the information the post office needs to deliver mail in a reasonably speedy fashion. Likewise, computer addresses have a structure to them. The general form is:

a person's email address on a computer: `user@somewhere.domain`
a computer's name: `somewhere.domain`

The *user* portion is usually the person's account name on the system, though it doesn't have to be;

`somewhere.domain` tells you the name of a system or location, and what kind of organization it is. The trailing *domain* is often one of the following:

com	Usually a company or other commercial institution or organization, like Cygnus Support (`cygnus.com`).
edu	An educational institution, for example, New York University, named `nyu.edu`.
gov	A government site; for example, NASA is `nasa.gov`.
mil	A military site, like the Air Force (`af.mil`).
net	Usually, gateways and other administrative hosts for a network (it does not mean all of the hosts in a network). `nic.near.net` and `nic.eu.net` are examples of these kinds of gateways.
org	A domain reserved for private organizations that don't comfortably fit in the other classes of domains. One example is the Electronic Frontier Foundation, named `eff.org`.

Each individual country also has its own top-level domain. For example, the `us` domain includes each of the fifty states (but is usually only used for small sites). Other countries represented with domains include:

au	Australia
ca	Canada
fr	France
ie	Ireland
uk	The United Kingdom. These also have subdomains separated by type; for example, `ac.uk` is used for academic sites and `co.uk` for commercial ones.

See Appendix F, *Country Codes*, for a full listing of the possible country domains. Note that even though a particular code is assigned to a country, that does not necessarily mean the country is connected to the Internet.

The proper terminology for a site's domain name, like the name *somewhere.domain* of the previous example, is its *Fully Qualified Domain Name*, or FQDN. It is usually selected to give a clear indication of the site's organization or sponsoring agent. For example, the Massachusetts Institute of Technology's FQDN is `mit.edu`; likewise, Apple Computer's domain name is `apple.com`. While such obvious names are usually the norm, there are the occasional exceptions that are ambiguous enough to mislead like `vt.edu`, which, on first impulse, one might surmise is an educational institution of some sort in Vermont; not so. It's actually the domain name for Virginia Tech. In most cases it's relatively easy to deduce the meaning of a domain name—such confusion is far from the norm.

Internet Numbers

 Every single machine on the Internet has a unique address,[1] called its *Internet number* or *IP Address*. It's actually a 32-bit number but is most commonly represented as four numbers joined by periods ('.'), like `147.31.254.130`. This is sometimes also called a *dotted quad*; there are literally thousands of different possible dotted quads. The ARPAnet (the mother of today's Internet) originally only had the capacity to have up to 256 systems on it because of the way each system was addressed. In the early '80s, it became clear that things would fast outgrow such a small limit; the 32-bit addressing method was born, freeing thousands of host numbers. However, there is growing concern that there may be a shortfall of addresses by the end of the twentieth century.

Each piece of an Internet address (like `192`) is called an *octet*, representing one of four sets of eight bits. The first two or three pieces (say `192.55.239`) represent the network that a system is on, called its *subnet*. For example, all of the computers for Wesleyan University are on the subnet `129.133`. They can have numbers like `129.133.10.10` and `129.133.230.19`, up to 65,000 possible combinations (possible computers).

IP addresses and domain names aren't assigned arbitrarily—that would lead to unbelievable confusion. An application must be filed with the InterNIC Registration Services, either electronically, by sending mail to `hostmaster@rs.internic.net`, or via regular mail.

---

1. At least one address, possibly two or even three—but we won't go into that.

Resolving Names and Numbers

OK, computers can be referred to by either their FQDN or their Internet address. How can you be expected to remember all those names?

You're not. The Internet is designed so that you can use either method. Since humans find it much more natural to deal with words than numbers, in most cases the FQDN for each host is mapped to its Internet number. Each domain is *served* by a computer within that domain, which provides all of the necessary information to go from a domain name to an IP address, and vice versa. For example, when someone refers to `foosun.bar.com`, the *resolver* knows that it should ask a certain system, say `foovax.bar.com`, about systems in the `bar.com` domain. If the name `foosun.bar.com` really exists, `foovax` will send `foosun`'s Internet address to the system that used it. All of this "magic" happens behind the scenes.

Rarely will you have to remember the Internet number of a site. However, you will remember a substantial number of FQDNs. It will eventually reach a point when you are able to make a reasonably accurate guess at what domain name a certain college, university, or company might have, given just its name.

The Networks

 Internet

The Internet is a large "network of networks." There is no one network known as The Internet; rather, regional nets like SuraNet, PrepNet, NearNet, etc. are all interconnected (nay, "internetworked") together into one great living thing, communicating at amazing speeds with the TCP/IP protocol. All activity takes place in "real time." The Internet offers mail, file transfer, remote login, and a plethora of other services.

▥➡ *UUCP*
The UUCP network is a loose association of systems all communicating with the UUCP protocol. (UUCP stands for Unix-to-Unix Copy Program.) It's based on two systems (e.g., *oregano* and *basil*) connecting to each other at specified intervals, called *polling*, and executing any work scheduled for either of them. Historically, most UUCP was done with Unix equipment, although the software has since been implemented on other platforms (including VMS and DOS). Let's say the system *oregano* polls the system *basil* once every two hours. If there's any mail waiting for *oregano*, *basil* will send it at that time; likewise, *oregano* will at that time send any jobs waiting for *basil*. Mail and Usenet news are the primary offerings of UUCP, although some general file transfer is available with the proper permission.

▥➡ *BITNET*
BITNET (the "Because It's Time Network") consists of systems connected by *point-to-point* links, all running the NJE protocol. Its growth has declined, as it finds itself suffering at the hands of the falling costs of Internet connections. Also, a number of mail gateways are in place to reach users on other networks. BITNET offers mail, mailing lists, and some file transfer but cannot support remote login. It is possible, though, to have interactive "discussions" with people on other machines. BITNET supports the ability to send a line of up to 160 characters to any user on any system.

The Physical Connection

The actual connections between the various networks take a variety of forms. The most common for Internet links are *56k leased lines* (dedicated telephone lines carrying 56 kilobit-per-second connections) and T1 (special) phone lines with 1 million bit-per-second connections).

Also installed are *T3 links*, acting as backbones between major locations to carry a massive load of traffic: 45 million bits per second. All of these numbers are rarely of concern to the typical user—things will just go very, very fast.

These links are paid for by each institution to a local carrier. Also available are *SLIP* or *PPP* connections, which carry Internet traffic (packets) over high-speed modems. If you dial up with your personal computer to do Web browsing, for example, you're probably using something like a SLIP connection.

UUCP links are made with modems (for the most part) that run from 1200 baud all the way up to as high as 28.8 Kbps. As was mentioned previously, the connections are of the *store-and-forward* variety. Also in use are Internet-based UUCP links. (As if things weren't already confusing enough!) The systems do their UUCP traffic over TCP/IP connections, which give the UUCP-based network some blindingly fast "hops," resulting in better connectivity for the network as a whole. UUCP connections first became popular in the '70s, and have remained in widespread use ever since.

The BITNET links that remain mostly take the form of 9600-bps modems connected from site to site. Often places have three or more links going; the majority, however, look to "upstream" sites for their sole link to the network.

"*The Glory and the Nothing of a Name*"
— Byron, "Churchill's Grave"

2 ELECTRONIC MAIL

The desire to communicate is the essence of networking. People have always wanted to correspond with each other in the fastest way possible, short of normal conversation. Electronic mail (or *email*) is the most prevalent application of this in computer networking. It allows people to write back and forth without having to spend much time worrying about how the message actually gets delivered. As technology grows closer and closer to being a common part of daily life, the need to understand the many ways it can be utilized and how it works, at least to some level, is vital.

Email Addresses

Electronic mail hinges on the concept of an *address*; the previous chapter made some reference to it while introducing domains. Your *email address* provides all of the information required to get a message to you from anywhere in the world. An address doesn't necessarily have to go to a human being. It could be an archive server,[1] a list of people, or even someone's pocket pager. These cases are the exception to the norm—mail to most addresses is read by human beings.

%@!.: Symbolic Cacophony

Email addresses usually appear in one of two forms— either in Internet format, which uses an "at" sign (the @ symbol), or in UUCP format, which uses an exclamation point (the ! symbol), which is sometimes referred to as a "bang." The latter, UUCP "bang" paths, tends to be more restrictive yet more clearly dictates how the mail will travel.

To reach Jim Morrison on the system `south.america.org`, you would address the mail as `jm@south.america.org`. But if Jim's account were on a UUCP site named *brazil*, then his address would be `brazil!jm`. If it's possible (and one exists), try to use the Internet form of an address; bang paths can fail if an intermediate site in the path happens to be down. There is a growing trend for UUCP sites to register Internet domain names to help alleviate the problem of path failures.

Another symbol that enters the fray is `%`—it acts as an extra "routing" method. For example, if the UUCP site `dream` is connected to `south.america.org` but doesn't have an Internet domain name of its own, a user named `debbie` on `dream` might be reached by writing to the address

```
debbie%dream@south.america.org
```

The form is significant. This address says that the local

---

1. See Appendix C, *Retrieving Files via Email*, to learn about archive servers.

system should first send the mail to `south.amer-ica.org`. The address `debbie%dream` will turn into `debbie@dream` on that system, which will hopefully be a valid address. Then, `south.america.org` will handle getting the mail to the host `dream`, where it will be delivered locally to `debbie`.

Many of the intricacies of email addressing methods are fully covered in the book *!%@:: A Directory of Electronic Mail Addressing and Networks,* published by O'Reilly and Associates as part of their Nutshell Handbook series. It is a must for any active email user. Write to `nuts@ora.com` for ordering information.

Anatomy of a Mail Header

An electronic mail message has a specific structure to it that's common across every type of computer system.[2] A possible message might be:

```
From bush@hq.mil Sat May 25 17:06:01 1991
Received: from hq.mil by house.gov with SMTP id
   AA21901 (4.1/SMI for dan@house.gov); Sat, 25
   May 91 17:05:56 -0400
Date: Sat, 25 May 91 17:05:56 -0400
From: The President <bush@hq.mil>
Message-Id: <9105252105.AA06631@hq.mil>
To: dan@senate.gov
Subject: Meeting

Hi Dan .. we have a meeting at 9:30 a.m. with the
Joint Chiefs. Please don't oversleep this time.
```

The first line with '`From`' and the two lines for '`Received:`' are usually not very interesting. They give the "real" address that the mail is coming from (as opposed to the address you should reply to, which may

---

2. The standard is written down in RFC-822. See page 154 for more info on how to get copies of the various RFCs.

look much different), and what places the mail went through to get to you. Over the Internet, there is always at least one 'Received:' header and usually no more than four or five. When a message is sent using UUCP, one 'Received:' header is added for each system that the mail passes through. This can often result in more than a dozen 'Received:' headers. While they help with dissecting problems in mail delivery, odds are that the average user will never want to see them. Most mail programs will filter out this kind of "cruft" in a header.

The 'Date:' header contains the date and time the message was sent. Likewise, the "good" address (as opposed to "real" address) is laid out in the 'From:' header. Sometimes it won't include the full name of the person (in this case, 'The President') and may look different, but it should always contain an email address of some form.

The message ID of a message is intended mainly for tracing mail routing and is rarely of interest to most users. Every message ID is guaranteed to be unique.

'To:' lists the email address (or addresses) of the recipients of the message. There may be a 'Cc:' header, listing additional addresses. Finally, a brief subject for the message goes in the 'Subject:' header.

The exact order of a message's headers may vary from system to system, but it will always include these fundamental headers, which are vital to proper delivery.

Bounced Mail

When an email address is incorrect in some way (the system's name is wrong, the domain doesn't exist, whatever), the mail system will *bounce* the message back to the sender, much the same way that the Postal

Service does when you send a letter to a bad street address. The message will include the reason for the bounce; a common error is addressing mail to an account name that doesn't exist. For example, writing to Lisa Simpson at Widener University's Computer Science department will fail, because she doesn't have an account.[3]

```
From: Mail Delivery Subsystem <MAILER-DAEMON>
Date: Sat, 25 May 91 16:45:14 -0400
To: mg@gracie.com (Matt Groening)
Cc: Postmaster@cs.widener.edu
Subject: Returned mail: User unknown


 --- Transcript of session follows ---
While talking to cs.widener.edu:
>>> RCPT To:<lsimpson@cs.widener.edu>
<<< 550 <lsimpson@cs.widener.edu>... User unknown
550 lsimpson... User unknown
```

As you can see, a carbon copy of the message (the 'Cc:' header entry) was sent to the postmaster of Widener's CS department. The *Postmaster* is responsible for maintaining a reliable mail system on his system or network. Usually, postmasters at sites will attempt to aid you in getting your mail where it's supposed to go. If a typing error was made, try sending the message again. If you're sure that the address is correct, contact the postmaster of the site directly and ask him for help in reaching the user.

The message also includes the text of the mail, so you don't have to retype everything you wrote.

---

3. Though if she asked, they'd certainly give her one.

Calvin and Hobbes

```
      ----- Unsent message follows -----
     Received: by cs.widener.edu id AA06528; Sat, 25
       May 91  16:45:14 -0400
     Date: Sat, 25 May 91 16:45:14 -0400
     From: Matt Groening <mg@gracie.com>
     Message-Id: <9105252045.AA06528@gracie.com>
     To: lsimpson@cs.widener.edu
     Subject: Scripting your future episodes
     Reply-To: writing-group@gracie.com

     . . .  etc . . .
```

The body of the message can be cut out with an editor and fed right back into the mail system with a proper address, making redelivery a relatively painless process.

Chain Letters In "real" life, a chain letter is one that promises good fortune if you copy and send a letter to some number of other people. People create email chain letters as well. They tend to cause nothing but damage to systems that are involved in them. If a chain letter is sent to five people and those five people each send it on to another five

by Bill Watterson

people, more than six hundred mail messages can be generated in less than an hour. Followed through, in one day a chain letter could generate over sixty thousand email messages. The effect of this kind of explosive traffic on a system which is intimately involved in it (e.g., many of the people passing the letters on send them to friends at school) can lead to disaster.

Indeed, MIT experienced just that—their main mail gateway was down for a period of time because students were repeatedly sending chain letters around. The problems caused by email chain letters cannot be emphasized enough: If you receive a chain letter, immediately report it to the postmaster of the system it came from. Chain letters stop being fun when no one at a site can receive mail because the mail queues are clogged.

Sending and Receiving Mail

We'll make one quick diversion from being OS-neuter here, to show you what it will look like to send and receive a mail message on a Unix system. There are *many* different mail programs for Unix alone, not to mention VMS and other systems. Check with your system administrator for specific instructions related to mail at your site.

A person sending mail would probably do something like this:

```
% mail sven@cs.widener.edu
Subject: print job's stuck


I typed `print babe.gif' and it didn't work! Why??
```

The next time Sven checked his mail, he would see it listed as

```
% mail
"/usr/spool/mail/sven": 1 messages 1 new 1 unread
U 1 joeuser@foo.widener Tue May 5 20:36 29/956 print
job's stuck
?
```

which gives information on the sender of the email, when it was sent, and the subject of the message. He would probably use the reply command of Unix mail to send this response:

```
? r
To: joeuser@foo.widener.edu
Subject: Re: print job's stuck


You shouldn't print binary files like GIFs to a printer!

Ciao.
```

Try sending yourself mail a few times to get used to your system's mailer. It'll save a lot of wasted aspirin for both you and those who may be paid to help you.

Mailing Lists

People who share common interests are inclined to discuss their hobby or interest at every available opportunity. One modern way to aid in this exchange of information is by using a *mailing list*—an email address that redistributes all mail sent to it back out to a list of addresses. For example, the Sun Managers mailing list (of interest to people that administer computers manufactured by Sun Microsystems) has the email address `sun-managers@eecs.nwu.edu`. Any mail sent to that address will "explode" out to each person named in a file maintained on a computer at Northwestern University.

Administrative tasks (sometimes referred to as *administrivia*) are often handled through other addresses, typically with the suffix '`-request`'. To continue the above, a request to be added to or deleted from the Sun Managers list should be sent to `sun-managers-request@eecs.nwu.edu`.

When in doubt, try to write to the '`-request`' version of a mailing list address first; the other people on the list aren't interested in your desire to be added or deleted and can certainly do nothing to expedite your request. Often, if the administrator of a list is busy (remember, this is all peripheral to real jobs and real work), many users find it necessary to ask again and again, often with harsher and harsher language, to be removed from a list. This does nothing more than cause traffic and bother everyone else receiving the messages. If, after a reasonable amount of time, you still haven't succeeded in being removed from a mailing list, write to the postmaster at that site and see if she can help.

Exercise caution when replying to a message sent by a mailing list. If you wish to respond to the author only, make *sure* that the only address you're replying to is that person, and not the entire list. Often messages such as "Yes, I agree with you completely!" will appear on a list, boring the daylights out of the other readers. Likewise, if you explicitly do want to send the message to the whole list, you'll save yourself some time by checking to make sure it's indeed headed to the whole list and not to a single person.

Stephanie da Silva (`arielle@taronga.com`) maintains the list of "Publicly Accessible Mailing Lists." Posted in separate portions to the newsgroup `news.lists` on a monthly basis, the list offers a fairly complete directory of the various lists you can join. (See Chapter 4, *Usenet News*, for info on how to read this and other newsgroups.)

Listservs

Originally started on BITNET, there's an automated system, called the *listserv*, for maintaining discussion lists. Rather than have an already harried and overworked human take care of additions and removals from a list, a program performs these and other tasks by responding to a set of user-driven commands.

Areas of interest are wide and varied—SF-LOVERS deals with fantasy and science fiction, while ADND-L has to do with a well-known role-playing game. A full list of the available lists housed on the BITNET listserv can be obtained by writing to `LISTSERV@BITNIC.CREN.NET`. In the body of the message, include the command

```
list global
```

However, be sparing in your use of this—find out if it's already on your system somewhere. The reply is quite large.

The most fundamental command is 'subscribe'. It will tell the listserv to add the sender to a specific list. The usage is

subscribe foo-l *Your Real Name*

It will respond with a message saying either that you've been added to the list or that the request has been passed on to the system on which the list is actually maintained.

To remove your address from a BITNET list, send the listserv

signoff foo-l

You will receive notification of the removal. If he or she is so inclined, the maintainer of the list may write you to ask if there's anything that displeased you about the mailing list that spurred your decision to leave it.

If you decide to leave *every* list, you can use the command

signoff global

This can be handy if your account is going to be turned off or if you discover it's interfering with your work. For a full list of the available listserv commands, write to LISTSERV@BITNIC.CREN.NET, giving it the command help.

American University maintains a *gateway* of every **BITNET** listserv list into the Usenet hierarchy bit.listserv. For cxample, SF-LOVERS is available as the Usenet newsgroup bit.listserv.ethics-l.

As an aside, there have been implementations of the listserv system for non-BITNET hosts (more specifically,

Unix systems). One of the more common is named Majordomo; it allows users to use the same syntax for adding and removing themselves from a list, among other features.

Pine Mail Program

A very popular and user-friendly program for sending and receiving email is *Pine*. Rather than operate in a flat-text, line-oriented manner, Pine provides the user with a full-screen display that looks and feels easier to use than its counterparts.[4]

To avoid confusion, Pine lists its options clearly at the bottom of each screen. Other mail programs assume the user can memorize the action corresponding to each keypress or expect them to remember multicharacter commands. Instead, users of Pine can start the program with the command `pine` and see immediately how to read and send their mail.

```
PINE 3.91 MAIN MENU      Folder: INBOX   9 Messages


    ?  HELP            Get help using Pine

    C  COMPOSE MESSAGE  Compose and send a message

    I  FOLDER INDEX View messages in current folder

    L  FOLDER LIST   Select a folder to view

    A  ADDRESS BOOK Update address book
```

4. The software for Pine, including prebuilt binaries for a variety of computers, is available via anonymous FTP from ftp.cac.washington.edu in the directory '/pine'.

```
    S  SETUP            Configure or update Pine

    Q  QUIT            - Exit the Pine program

Copyright 1989-1994.  PINE is a trademark of the
University of Washington.
      [Folder "INBOX" opened with 9 messages]
? Help          P PrevCmd      R RelNotes
O OTHER CMDS    L [ListFldrs]N NextCmd   K KBLock
```

The first Pine screen lists the basic functions: look-ing at the index of their current mail folder (having mul-tiple folders is an option users can take advantage of after they're comfortable with the program), how to write, or "compose," email, and how to quit out of the program. And online help is always available simply by typing '?'.

While Pine presents itself as a simple tool, it is still a very powerful one. Features like saving mail to a spe-cific folder (e.g., saving all the mail related to a certain project to a separate mail file) are there for the users' exploration at their leisure. Pine also sports the ability to *postpone* a message. Pine you want to send mail to someone but get interrupted in the middle of writing it, you don't need to delete what you've just written and start over again when the time is available. When you postpone a message with Pine, it will save a copy of what you've done and let you continue it later. Each time you try to 'c'ompose a new message, Pine will ask if you'd like to finish any postponed messages.

Pine also supports the idea of having an online "address book." This makes it possible for users to have to know someone's full email address just once—after they've put it in their address book, they need only recall a single word that acts as the equivalent of the address. For example, to send mail to Kevin Arnold at `imlucid@eworld.com`, you would put his address into the address book with the word "`beavis`" as its match. Thus, whenever you wished to send mail to him, you would only have to type the word "`beavis`" in the '`To:`' field, and Pine would automatically fill out the full address.

If you're nervous about learning all of the details of the `mail` command or a similar tool, Pine may prove to be an easier entrance into the world of electronic mail. If typing `pine` doesn't work on the system you've logged in to, ask your system administrator or your support staff to install it for you.

Some Fun with Email: The Oracle

Steve Kinzler of Indiana University and Ray Moody, then of Purdue University, created a truly novel utility on the Net: the Usenet Oracle. Despite its name, the Oracle doesn't have much to do with Usenet (aside from being gatewayed into the group `rec.humor.oracle` in the form of the *Usenet Oracularities*).[5]

You can use the Oracle by writing to the following email address: `oracle@cs.indiana.edu`. If you'd like more information about the Oracle, including historical background on the ancient Oracle of Delphi, send your mail with a '`Subject:`' line containing the word '`help`'.

To ask the Oracle a question, your '`Subject:`' line should contain the phrase "tell me". For example, a typical question might look like the following; be as creative as you can.

---

5. See "Reading News" on page 42 of the *Usenet News* chapter to find out how to read the newsgroup.

```
To: oracle@cs.indiana.edu
Subject: Oracle Most Wise, please tell me ...

O Wise Oracle, whose party gags are always
funny, even if they involve lampshades, and
whose pickup lines are always successful, even
if they involve the zodiac, please enlighten
your supplicant on the following:

What is the best pickup line in history?
```

As you can see, the Oracle is not intended to be used for serious questions. Embellishment before you ask your question can help make it even more entertaining.

In answer, you will receive a message with a response from the Oracle. As "payment" for the privilege of using the Oracle, you may be asked to answer someone else's question.

In response to the question it received, the Oracle might reply with

```
Date: Mon, 06 Sep 93 10:08:24 -0500
From: Usenet Oracle <oracle@cs.indiana.edu>

The Usenet Oracle has pondered your question
deeply.Your question was:

> O Wise Oracle, . . .
>
> What is the best pickup line in history?

And in response, thus spake the Oracle:

] The best pickup line in history is, of course,
} FORD.
}
} You owe the Oracle one 1993 Ford F350 with all
} the extras.
```

Getting the jokes in the Oracle's replies is left as an exercise for the reader.

If you want to read some of the previous answers and laugh quitc a bit, FTP to `cs.indiana.edu` and look in the directory '`/pub/oracle`'. To understand how to use FTP, continue reading to the next chapter. If you don't have the ability to take advantage of FTP, you can write to the address `mailserv@cs.indiana.edu` with "`help`" in the body of the message. You will reive the instructions on how to retrieve the various Oracle files via email.

"I made this letter longer than usual because I lack the time to make it shorter."

— Pascal, *Provincial Letters XVI*

3 ANONYMOUS FTP

FTP (the *File Transfer Protocol*) is the primary method of transferring files over the Internet. On many systems, it's also the name of the program that implements the protocol. Given proper permission, it's often possible to copy a file from a computer in South Africa to one in Los Angeles at very fast speeds (on the order of 5–10K per second). This normally requires either a user ID on both systems or a special configuration set up by the system administrator(s).

There is a good way around this restriction—the *anonymous FTP* service. It essentially will let anyone in the world have access to a certain area of disk space in a nonthreatening way. With this, people can make files publicly available with little hassle. Some systems have dedicated entire disks or even entire computers to maintaining extensive archives of source code and information. They include `ftp.uu.net` (UUNET), `wuarchive.wustl.edu` (Washington University in Saint Louis), and `archive.cis.ohio-state.edu` (The Ohio State University).

The process involves the "foreign" user (someone not on the system itself) creating an FTP connection and logging in to the system as the user 'anonymous', with an arbitrary password:

```
Name (foo.site.com:you): anonymous
Password: jm@south.america.org
```

Custom and "netiquette" dictate that people respond to the 'Password:' query with an email address so that the sites can track the level of FTP usage, if they desire. (See page 9 for information on email addresses.)

The speed of the transfer depends on the speed of the underlying link. A site that has a 9600 baud SLIP connection will not get the same throughput as a system with a T1 leased line. (See page 7 for more information on what kinds of connections can exist in a network.) Also, the traffic of all other users on that link will affect performance. If there are 30 people all FTPing from one site simultaneously, the load on the system (in addition to the network connection) will degrade the overall throughput of the transfer.

FTP Etiquette

Lest we forget, the Internet is there for people to do their work. People using the network and the systems on it are doing so for a purpose, whether it be research, development, or whatever. Any heavy activity takes away from the overall performance of the network as a whole.

The effects of an FTP connection on a site and its link can vary; the general rule of thumb is that any extra traffic detracts from the ability of that site's users to perform their tasks. To be considerate of this, it's *highly* recommended that FTP sessions be held only after normal business hours for that site, preferably late at night. The possible effects of a large transfer will be less destructive at 2 a.m. than at 2 p.m. Also, remember that if it's past dinner time in Maine, it's still early afternoon in California—think in terms of the current time at the site that's being visited, not your local time.

Basic Commands

While there have been many extensions to the various FTP clients out there, there is a de facto "standard" set that everyone expects to work. For more information, read the manual for your FTP program. This section will only skim the bare minimum of commands needed to operate an FTP session.

Creating the Connection

The actual command to use FTP will vary among operating systems; for the sake of clarity, we'll use `ftp` here, since it's the most common.

There are two ways to connect to a system—using its *hostname* or its Internet number. Using the hostname is usually preferred. However, some sites aren't able to *resolve* hostnames properly and have no alternative. We'll assume you're able to use hostnames, for simplicity's sake. Contact your local administrator or support staff for tips on getting around any local restrictions or problems.

The form of the command is:

```
ftp somewhere.domain
```

See "The Physical Connection" on page 7 for help with reading and using domain names (*somewhere.domain* is the system `archive.cis.ohio-state.edu` in the example below).

You must first know the name of the system you

want to connect to. We'll choose the archive of Ohio State University. On your system, type:

```
ftp archive.cis.ohio-state.edu
```

(The actual syntax will vary, depending on the type of system the connection's being made from.) The system will pause momentarily, then respond with the message

```
Connected to archive.cis.ohio-state.edu.
```

and an initial prompt will appear:

```
220 archive FTP server (Version wu-2.4(2) Mon Apr 18 14:41:30 EDT 1994) ready.
Name (archive.cis.ohio-state.edu:jm):
```

to which you should respond with `anonymous`:

```
220 archive FTP server (Version wu-2.4(2) Mon Apr 18 14:41:30 EDT 1994) ready.
Name (archive.cis.ohio-state.edu:jm): anonymous
```

The system will then prompt you for a password; as noted previously, a good response is your email address:

```
331 Guest login ok, send your complete e-mail address as password.
Password: jm@south.america.org
230 Guest login ok, access restrictions apply.
ftp>
```

The password itself will not echo. This is to protect a user's security when he or she is using a real account to FTP files between machines. Once you reach the 'ftp>' prompt, you know you're logged in and ready to go.

Be careful when you answer the 'Password:' prompt! Do not, under any circumstances, use your real system password when using anonymous FTP. There is no reason for a remote system to need your local password. Give only your email address, unless the remote system requires you to type a generic password like '`guest`'.

Sometimes a system will have a limit on the number of users it can have doing anonymous FTP at the same time; if that's the case, you may encounter a message asking you to try again later, instead of receiving the '`Password:`' prompt. If this is the case, you usually only need to wait for a few minutes before another FTP connection will let you on.

dir: Directory of Files

At the '`ftp>`' prompt, you can type a number of commands to perform various functions. One example is `dir`—it will list the files in the current directory. Continuing the example from above:

```
ftp> dir
200 PORT command successful.
150 Opening ASCII mode data connection for /bin/ls.
total 763
-rw-r-----  1 5     5        0 Dec 18  1991 .hushlogin
drwxr-sr-x  3 216   274    512 Jan 19  1993 Usenix
drwxrwsr-x  2 482   274   1536 Oct 28  1994 X-contrib
                    ... etc ...
-rw-r--r--  1 root 274   327853 May  2 08:39 ls-lR.Z
-rw-r--r--  1 root 274   327879 May  1 08:39 ls-lR.Z-OLD
                    ... etc ...
drwxr-sr-x 11 2112 274    512 May  2 16:47 tech-report
drwxrwxr-x  2 2015 268    512 Jun 18  1994 tensor
drwxrwsr-x  3 root 274    512 Apr 23  1994 tex
drwxr-sr-x  6 5004 274   1024 Mar  1 21:32 tknews
drwxrwsr-x  2 root 10     512 Jul 28  1994 tmp
drwxr-sr-x  2 216  274    512 Apr 23  1994 update-servers
drwxrwsr-x  2 2134 274    512 Jul 15  1994 w3browser
drwxrwsr-x  3 216  274    512 Mar 21 22:12 www
drwxr-sr-x 13 5063 274    512 Apr 29 06:17 yagel
226 Transfer complete.
ftp>
```

The file 'ls-lR.Z' was specifically included because we'll
be using it later. Just for general information, this file in
particular, when a site creates it, is used to contain a listing of all the files in the archive.

The directory shown is on a machine running the
Unix operating system; the `dir` command will produce
different results on other operating systems (like MS-
DOS, VMS, etc.). Learning to recognize different formats will take some time. After a few weeks of travers-
ing the Internet, it proves easier to see, for example,
how large a file is on an operating system you're otherwise not acquainted with.

With many FTP clients, it's also possible to take the
output of `dir` and put it into a file on the local system
with

```
ftp> dir l* outfilename
```

The results can then be read outside the live FTP connection; this is particularly useful for systems with very long
directory listings (like `archive.cis.ohio-state.edu`).
The above example would put the name of every file that
begins with the letter 'l' into the local file 'outfilename'.

cd:
Changing
the Current
Directory

When you begin of an FTP session, you start at a "top-
level" directory. Most things are in directories below it
(e.g., '/pub' is a common first step). To change the current directory, one uses the `cd` command. To change to
the directory 'pub' that we saw above, type

```
ftp> cd pub
```

which would elicit the response

```
250 CWD command successful.
```

meaning that the "Change Working Directory" command (`cd`) worked properly.

Keep in mind that many systems are case-sensitive; the directory or file '`Test`' is often different from '`test`'. If you get in the practice of doing things in lower case, you'll meet with a high degree of success.

From the new directory, typing `dir` again will list the files (and, possibly, other subdirectories) available for FTP in that directory. You'll now see '`ls-lR.Z`', a compressed file listing all of the files available from the system. Note that files like this, if they have been created, can often be quite large. (This example is over 300 kilobytes in size.) Only get it if you really need to see the heavy listing instead of just moving around the directories by hand, looking for the file you're after.[1]

get and put:
File Transfer

The actual transfer is performed with the `get` and `put` commands. To *get* a file from the remote computer to the local system, use the command

        ftp> get *filename*

where *filename* is the file on the remote system. Continuing our session with Ohio State, the file '`ls-lR.Z`' can be retrieved with

```
ftp> get ls-lR.Z
200 PORT command successful.
150 Opening ASCII mode data connection for ls-lR.Z (327853 bytes).
226 Transfer complete.
329124 bytcs received in 16 seconds (20 Kbytes/s)
ftp>
```

1. Skip ahead to "The Archie Server" on page 35 to learn how to find specific files more quickly.

The section below on using binary mode instead of ASCII will describe why this particular choice will result in a corrupt and subsequently unusable file.

If, for some reason, you want to save a file under a different name (e.g., your system can only have 14-character filenames or can only have one dot in the name), you can specify what the local filename should be by providing `get` with an additional argument

```
ftp> get update-servers  update
```

which will place the contents of the file '`update-servers`' in the filename '`update`' on the local system. This is handy for systems like VMS and MS-DOS, which have restrictions on what a filename can look like. For example, if you try to get a file with more than one period in it (e.g., '`foo.tar.z`') while using FTP from a system running VMS or MS-DOS, you will receive an error about an incorrect filename. To avoid this problem, you can use a local filename that has only one period in it:

```
ftp> get foo.tar.Z foo-tar.Z
```

Transfers work the other way, too. The `put` command will transfer a file from the local system to the remote system. If the permissions are set up for an FTP session to write to a remote directory, a file can be sent with

```
ftp> put filename
```

As with `get`, `put` will take a second argument, letting you specify a different name for the file on the remote system.

ASCII vs. Binary

In the previous example, the file '1s-1R.Z' was transferred, but supposedly not correctly. The reason is this: In a normal ASCII transfer (the default), certain characters are translated between systems to help make text files more readable. However, when *binary* files—those containing non-ASCII characters—are transferred, this translation should *not* take place. One example is a binary program: A few changed characters can render it completely useless.

To avoid this problem, it's possible to be in one of two modes—*ASCII* or *binary*. In binary mode, the file isn't translated in any way. What's on the remote system is precisely what's received. The commands to go between the two modes are:

```
ftp> ascii
200 Type set to A.    (Note the A, which signifies ASCII mode.)


ftp> binary
200 Type set to I.    (Set to Image format, for pure binary transfers.)
```

Note that each command need be done only once to take effect; if the user types `binary`, all transfers in that session are done in binary mode (that is, unless `ascii` is typed later).

The transfer of '1s-1R.Z' will work if done as:

```
ftp> binary
200 Type set to I.
ftp> get 1s-1R.Z
200 PORT command successful.
150 Opening BINARY mode data connection for 1s-1R.Z (327853 bytes).
226 Transfer complete.
local: 1s-1R.Z remote: 1s-1R.Z
327853 bytes received in 18 seconds (17 Kbytes/s)
```

Note: The file size (327853) is different from that done in
ASCII mode (329124 bytes); and the number 327853
matches the one we were told at the beginning of the
BINARY transfer. We can be relatively sure that we've
received the file without any problems.

mget and mput: Multiple Files

The commands `mget` and `mput` allow for multiple file
transfers, using wildcards to get several files or a whole
set of files at once, rather than having to do it manually,
one by one. For example, to get all files that begin with
the letter '`f`', you would type

```
ftp> mget f*
```

Similarly, to put all of the local files that end with '`.c`':

```
ftp> mput*.c
```

Rather than me reiterating what's been written a
hundred times before, consult a local manual for more
information on wildcard matching (every DOS manual,
for example, has a section on it).

Normally, FTP assumes that a user wants to be
prompted for every file in an `mget` or `mput` operation.
You'll often need to get a whole set of files and not have
each of them confirmed—you know they're all right. In
that case, use the `prompt` command to turn the queries
off.

```
ftp> prompt
Interactive mode off.
```

Likewise, to turn queries back on, simply reissue the
`prompt` command.

Those '.Z' Files

A large number of the FTP sites around the world are running the Unix operating system. To conserve space, files are often "compressed" to a smaller, more compact size. The Unix utility (called `compress`) that performs this operation gives the new file a '`.z`' extension. To restore the file to its original size (so you can use it), use the `uncompress` command on a Unix system. If you're on a system running VMS, use the public domain program called `LZDCM`; versions of `uncompress` have also been ported to MS-DOS. For other operating systems, consult the manual for it or contact your local system administrator or support staff for assistance.

The *Archie* Server

A group of people at McGill University in Canada got together and created a query system called *Archie*. It was originally formed to be a quick and easy way to scan the offerings of the many anonymous FTP sites that are maintained around the world. As time progressed, Archie grew to include other valuable services as well. Its inventors formed a company (see page 113) to meet the rising demand for faster and more stable Archie servers and professional support.

The Archie databases are accessible through an interactive telnet session, email queries, WWW forms, as well as command-line and X Window clients. The email responses can be used along with FTPmail servers for those not on the Internet. (See Appendix C, *Retrieving Files via Email*, for information on using FTPmail servers.)

Using Archie *Today*

Currently, Archie tracks the contents of over 1200 anonymous FTP archive sites containing over five million files stored across the Internet. Collectively, these files represent well over 50 gigabytes of information, with new entries being added daily.

The Archie server automatically updates the listing information from each site about twice a month. This avoids constantly updating the databases, which could waste network resources, yet ensures that the information on each site's holdings is reasonably up-to-date.

As the information available on each Archie server is identical, it is more convenient and more effective to access the closest server when performing a query. To access Archie interactively, telnet to one of the many servers around the world.[2]

Australia	archie.au
Austria	archie.univie.ac.at
Belgium	archie.belnet.be
Canada	archie.bunyip.com
	archie.cs.mcgill.ca
	archie.uqam.ca
Finland	archie.funet.fi
France	archie.univ-rennes1.fr
Germany	archie.th-darmstadt.de
Israel	archie.ac.il
Italy	archie.unipi.it

2. See Chapter 5, *Telnet* for notes on using the `telnet` program.

Japan	archie.wide.ad.jp
Korea	archie.hana.nm.kr
	archie.sogang.ac.kr
New Zealand	archie.nz
Norway	archie.uninett.no
Poland	archie.icm.edu.pl
Spain	archie.rediris.es
Sweden	archie.luth.se
Switzerland	archie.switch.ch
Taiwan	archie.ncu.edu.tw
United Kingdom	archie.doc.ic.ac.uk
	archie.hensa.ac.uk
USA *(Maryland)*	archie.sura.net
(Nebraska)	archie.unl.edu
(New York the InterNIC)	archie.internic.net
(New Jersey)	archie.rutgers.edu

At the 'login:' prompt of one of the servers, enter 'archie'—it won't ask for a password. A greeting will be displayed, detailing information about ongoing work in the Archie project; the user will be left at an 'archie>' prompt, which takes the interactive commands. Typing help will yield instructions on using the prog command to make queries, set will control various aspects of the session, and so on. The list of Archie servers may change over time. To receive the most up-to-date list of possible servers, use the command `servers` to list those currently available. Typing `quit` at the prompt will leave Archie.

The query "`prog vine.tar.Z`" will yield a list of the systems that offer the source to the X Windows program `vine`; a piece of the information returned looks like:

```
Host qiclab.scn.rain.com    (204.188.34.97)
Last updated 01:18 20 May 1995

 Location: /pub/X11
   FILE    -rw-r--r--   16112 bytes  20:00  8 Jun 1991  vine.tar.Z


          ... etc ...


 Host ftp.cc.utexas.edu    (128.83.40.1)
Last updated 06:37 18 Jun 1995

 Location: /source/games
    FILE    -rw-r--r--   12019 bytes  20:00  6 May 1988  vine.tar.Z
```

Archie Clients

Many Archie clients exist for performing Archie queries, but there are two mainstream clients, one called (naturally enough) '`archie`', the other '`xarchie`' (for X Windows). They query the Archie databases and yield a list of systems that have the requested file(s) available for anonymous FTP without requiring an interactive session to the server. For example, to find similar information to what you tried with the server command `prog`, you could type

```
% archie vine.tar.Z
 Host ftp.cc.utexas.edu

  Location: /source/games
    FILE -rw-r--r--  12019  May  7 1988  vine.tar.Z


          ... etc ...
```

```
Host ftp.center.osaka-u.ac.jp

  Location: /X-contrib
    FILE -r--r--r-- 15548  Oct 31 1991  vine.tar.Z
```

Note that your system administrator may not have installed the Archie clients yet; the source is available on each of the Archie servers, in the directory `archie/clients`.

Using the X Windows client is much more intuitive—if it's installed, just read its man page and give it a whirl. It's essential for the networked desktop.

With the growing use of the World Wide Web as a means for surfing the Internet, Archie query gateways were written to allow users to make Archie queries by using a form-based Web page.[3] The URL for one of the pages offering this type of search is

```
http://services.bunyip.com:8000/products/archie
```

Also available on the Web is the list of current servers, as you'd receive with the 'servers' command when you telnet into an Archie server; the URL for this list is:

```
http://services.bunyip.com:8000/products/archie/archiemap.html
```

Mailing Archie

Users limited to email connectivity to the Internet should send a message to the address `archie@archie.bunyip.com` with the single word "`help`" in the body of the message. An email message will be returned, explaining how to use the email

3. See "Using the Web" on page 78 to learn how to browse the World Wide Web.

Archie server—most of the commands offered by the telnet interface are available.

The same rules hold with email requests as with use of the telnet interface. If you pick an Archie server that's close to you, the turn-around time for a query will be very short.

Gopher Space

The design of the Archie system was orchestrated so it could be easily extended to include other databases—not just lists of FTP sites. Hence, in addition to the anonymous FTP database, the Archie system also has a Gopher database, which is populated by indexing registered sites. Not every Archie server offers the Gopher database. To learn more about gopher in general, see "The Internet Gopher" on page 101.

More Information on Archie

As with other services, Archie has continued to grow at a fairly rapid pace over a short period of time. For more detailed and recent information about Archie, use your Web browser to visit the URL

```
http://services.bunyip.com:8000/products/archie
```

Mail describing your ideas for additional databases and suggested improvements for increasing Archie's ease of use are welcome. To contact the Archie developers, write to `archie-group@bunyip.com`.

"Was für ein Platz zum plündern!"
("What a place to plunder!")
— Gebhard Leberecht Blücher

4 USENET NEWS

The first thing to understand about Usenet is that it is widely misunderstood. Every day on Usenet the "blind men and the elephant" phenomenon appears, in spades. In my opinion, more *flame wars* (rabid arguments) arise because of a lack of understanding of the nature of Usenet than from any other source. And consider that such flame wars arise, of necessity, among people who are on Usenet. Imagine, then, how poorly understood Usenet must be by those outside!

Usenet Basics

One of the first approaches to communications on what became the Internet took the form of Usenet *newsgroups*. These "discussion areas" are a style of passive exchange of information between interested parties. A newsgroup is a collection of messages on a particular topic; there are thousands and thousands of them, varying in subject from car maintenance to the discussion of a particular culture. In essence, if there is a subject you're interested in talking about, there's probably a newsgroup dedicated to it.

In contrast to messages distributed on mailing lists, postings to a newsgroup are stored in a common area and require that the user actively pursue reading them. A message you post to a group is then passed on to other sites, which in turn distribute it even further. This teamwork eventually leads to your words being available to be read on systems around the world.

Beware, though: It's easy to underestimate the amount of time this could take out of your day. Many find themselves perusing post after post, actually retaining little of what they've looked at. There is a plethora of information in Usenet news, and it will take some effort to find what you can really use.

Reading News

How you actually access Usenet newsgroups varies dramatically from one system to another. On Unix systems alone, there are at least seven different news readers you can use. Your best bet is to ask your support staff or system administrator how to read news on your local system. If you are reading news independently of work or school, the service you're using probably has either an online help facility or some sort of printed documentation.

Under Unix, `rn`, `trn`, and `nn` are common news readers. With VMS, the command is often NEWS. Many personal computers that are connected to the Internet have news readers available at the click of an icon. Some readers present everything in a single color and font, while others present each posting with certain portions in bold or italic. The base content of the article, the person's words, is the same from site to site.

Common to all news readers is a list of groups that you want to read. This list can be very large (in excess of 5,000 groups in many cases); don't start to blink in wonder and question why you even bothered trying. Most of these files have a sensible format to them, and you can "unsubscribe" to everything at once, and then subscribe only to the things you're really interested in.

For example, most Unix newsreaders use a '.newsrc' file, which lists each group with either a colon (you're subscribed) or an exclamation point (you're not) after the name. Using your favorite text editor, you should be able to replace all of the colons with exclamation points and then start trolling down the list, picking things you think you might be interested in. On your home computer, the news reader probably has a point-and-click tool you can use to choose and exclude groups. Similarly, many online services, including America Online, have a graphic interface you can use to choose the groups you want to read.

Bogus Newsgroups Occasionally, people will take advantage of the Usenet newsgroup mechanism and create "fake" newsgroups. They have included names like `alt.swedish-chef.bork.bork.bork`. While they can occasionally be funny, they cause no small amount of grief for news administrators. If you do figure out how to fake a control message to create a group, just pride yourself on your ingenuity—you and everyone else will be much happier.

Hierarchies

Newsgroups are organized according to their specific areas of concentration. Since the groups are in a *tree* structure, the various areas are called hierarchies. There are seven major categories:

comp	Topics of interest to both computer professionals and hobbyists, including topics in computer science, software sources, and information on hardware and software systems.
misc	Groups that are neither fish nor fowl usually end up being part of the misc hierarchy. Subjects include fitness, job-hunting, law, and investments.
sci	Discussions marked by special knowledge relating to research in or application of the established sciences.
soc	Groups primarily addressing social issues and socializing. Included are discussions related to many different world cultures.
talk	Groups largely debate-oriented and tending to feature long discussions without resolution and without appreciable amounts of generally useful information.

news	Groups concerned with the news network, group maintenance, and software.
rec	Groups oriented toward hobbies and recreational activities.

These "world" newsgroups are (usually) circulated around the entire Usenet—this implies worldwide distribution. Not all groups actually enjoy such wide distribution, however. The European Usenet and Eunet sites take only a selected subset of the more "technical" groups, and controversial "noise" groups are often not carried by many sites in the U.S. and Canada (these groups are primarily under the 'talk' and 'soc' classifications). Many sites do not carry some or all of the comp.binaries groups because of the typically large size of the posts in them (being actual executable programs).

Also available are a number of "alternative" hierarchies:

alt	True anarchy; anything and everything can and does appear; subjects include sex, new television shows, and privacy.
gnu	Groups concentrating on interests and software with the GNU Project of the Free Software Foundation.
biz	Business-related groups.

Each is selectively carried or denied on a site and often constitute a majority of the overall traffic that occurs in receiving the groups. For example, the alt.sex news hierarchy has proven to have the highest levels of content among all the newsgroups. In fact, one portion of this hierarchy, distributing graphic images that are often quite explicit, has been the source of much controversy.

Moderated vs. Unmoderated

Some newsgroups insist that the discussion remain focused and on target; to serve this need, moderated groups were invented. All articles posted to a moderated group get mailed to the group's *moderator*. He or she periodically (hopefully sooner than later) reviews the posts, then either posts them individually to Usenet or posts a composite *digest* of the articles for the past day or two. This is how many mailing list gateways work (e.g., the *Risks Digest*).

news.groups and news.announce.newgroups

Being a good *net.citizen* includes being involved in the continuing growth and evolution of the Usenet system. One part of this involvement includes following the discussion in `news.groups` and `news.announce.newgroups`. It is there that discussion goes on about the creation of new groups and the destruction of inactive ones. Every person on Usenet is allowed and encouraged to vote on the creation of a newsgroup.

Weekly, the moderator of `news.announce.newgroups` posts updates detailing the votes that are running, those that have passed, and other information. By reading these, you can stay informed and do not need to wade through the usually high-traffic `news.groups`.

How Usenet Works

The transmission of Usenet news is entirely cooperative. Feeds are generally provided out of good will and the desire to distribute news everywhere. There are places that provide feeds for a fee (e.g., UUNET), but for the large part no exchange of money is involved.

There are two major transport methods, UUCP and NNTP. The first is mainly modem-based and involves the normal charges for telephone calls. The second, NNTP, is the primary method for distributing news over the Internet.

With UUCP, news is stored in *batches* on a site until the neighbor calls to receive the articles or until the feed site happens to call. A list of groups that the neighbor wishes to receive is maintained on the feed site. The Cnews system compresses its batches, which can dramatically reduce the transmission time necessary for a relatively heavy newsfeed.

NNTP, on the other hand, offers a little more latitude with how news is sent. The traditional store-and-forward method is, of course, available. Given the real-time nature of the Internet, though, other methods have been devised. Programs now keep constant connections with their news neighbors, sending news nearly instantaneously, and can handle dozens of simultaneous feeds, both incoming and outgoing.

The transmission of a Usenet article is centered around the unique `Message-ID:` header. When an NNTP site offers an article to a neighbor, it says it has that specific Message ID. If the neighbor finds it hasn't received the article yet, it tells the feed to send it through; this is repeated for each and every article that's waiting for the neighbor. Using unique IDs helps prevent a system from receiving five copies of an article from each of its five news neighbors, for example.

Mail Gateways

A natural progression is for Usenet news and electronic mailing lists to somehow become merged—which they have, in the form of *news gateways*. Many mailing lists are set up to "reflect" messages not only to the readership of the list, but also into a newsgroup. Likewise, posts to a newsgroup can be sent to the moderator of the mailing list or to the entire mailing list. Some examples of this in action are `comp.risks` (the *Risks Digest*) and `comp.dcom.telecom` (the *Telecom Digest*).

This method of propagating mailing-list traffic has helped solve the problem of a single message being delivered to a number of people at the same site—instead, anyone can just subscribe to the group. Also, mailing list maintenance is lowered substantially, since the moderators don't have to be constantly removing and adding users to and from the list. Instead, people can read the newsgroup at their leisure.

Usenet "Netiquette"

There are many traditions with Usenet, not the least of which is dubbed *netiquette*—being polite and considerate of others. If you follow a few basic guidelines, you, and everyone that reads your posts, will be much happier in the long run.

Signatures

At the end of most articles is a small blurb called a person's *signature*, or just "sig." In Unix this file is named '`.signature`' in the person's login directory—the name

will vary for other operating systems. Sig exists to provide information about how to get in touch with the person posting the article, including an email address,
phone number, address, or location Even so, signatures
have become the graffiti of computers. People put song
lyrics, pictures, philosophical quotes, and even advertisements in their ".sigs." (Note, however, that advertising in your signature will more often than not get you
flamed until you take it out.)

Four lines will suffice—more is just extra garbage
for Usenet sites to carry along with your article, which
is supposed to be the intended focus of the reader. Netiquette dictates limiting oneself to this "quota" of
four—some people make signatures that are ten lines
or even more, including elaborate ASCII drawings of
their hand-written signature or faces or even the space
shuttle. This is not cute and will bother people to no
end.

The newsgroup `alt.fan.warlord` is a dumping
ground for the most heinous of signature violations. In
the course of reading news, people occasionally do follow-ups into `alt.fan.warlord` to show off their latest discoveries—talking whales, ten-line-high cacti, and a
variety of other ASCII miracles.

It's also not absolutely necessary to include a signature—if you forget to append it to an article, *don't worry
about it*. The article's just as good as it ever would be
and contains everything you should want to say. Don't
re-post the article just to make sure people see your sig.

*Posting
Personal
Messages*

If mail to a person doesn't make it through, avoid posting the message to a newsgroup. Even if the likelihood
of that person reading the group is very high, all the
other people reading the articles don't give a whit what

you have to say to Jim Morrison. Simply wait for the person to post again and double-check the address or get in touch with your system administrator and see if it's a problem with local email delivery. It may also turn out that the person's site is down or is having problems, in which case it's just necessary to wait until things return to normal before contacting Jim.

Posting Mail   In the interests of privacy, it's considered extremely bad taste to post any email that someone may have sent, unless they explicitly give you permission to redistribute it. While the legal issues can be heavily debated, almost everyone agrees that email should be treated as anything one would receive via normal snailmail,[1] preserving all of the assumed rights it carries.

Test Messages   Many people, particularly new users, want to try out posting before actually taking part in discussions. Often, the mechanics of getting messages out is the most difficult part of Usenet. To this end, many, many users find it necessary to post their tests to "normal" groups (for example, `news.admin` or `comp.mail.misc`). This is considered a major netiquette faux pas in the Usenet world. There are a number of groups available, called *test groups*, which exist solely for the purpose of trying out a news system, reader, or even new signature. They include:

```
alt.test
gnu.gnusenet.test
misc.test
```

some of which will generate *auto-magic* replies to your posts to let you know they made it through. There are

---

1. The slang for the normal land and air postal service.

certain denizens of Usenet who frequent the test groups to help new users out. They respond to the posts, often including the article so the poster can see how it got to the person's site. Also, many regional hierarchies have test groups, like `phl.test` in Philadelphia.

By all means, experiment and test—just do it in its proper place.

Famous People Appearing

Every once in a while, someone says that a celebrity is accessible through the Net; or, even more entertaining, an article is forged to appear to be coming from that celebrity. One example of this is with Stephen Spielberg— the `rec.arts.movies` readership was in an uproar for two weeks following a couple of posts supposedly made by Mr. Spielberg. (Some detective work revealed it to be a hoax.)

There are a few well-known people who are acquainted with Usenet and networks in general—but the overwhelming majority are just normal people. One should act with skepticism whenever a notable personality is "seen" in a newsgroup.

Summaries

Authors of articles occasionally say that readers should reply by mail and they'll *summarize*. Accordingly, readers should do just that—reply via mail. Responding with a follow-up article to such an article defeats the intention of the author. In a few days, he will post one article containing the highlights of the responses he received. If you follow up to the whole group, the author may not read what you have to say.

When creating a summary of the replies to a post, try to make it as *reader friendly* as possible. Avoid just putting all of the messages received into one big file. Rather, take some time and edit the messages into a form that contains only the essential information that other readers would be interested in.

Sometimes people will respond but request to remain anonymous (one example might be employees who feel the information's not proprietary but at the same time want to protect themselves from political backlash in their company). Summaries should honor this request accordingly by listing the 'From:' address as "anonymous" or "(Address withheld by request)'.'

Quoting   When following up on an article, many newsreaders provide the facility to *quote* the original article with each line prefixed by '>', as in

```
In article <1232@foo.bar.com>,
sharon@foo.bar.com wrote:
> I agree, I think that basketweaving's really
> catching on, particularly in Pennsylvania.
> Here's a list of every person
> in PA that currently engages in it publicly:
       . . . etc . . .
```

This is a severe example (potentially a horribly long article) but proves a point. When you quote another person, *edit out* whatever isn't directly applicable to your reply.[2] This gives the reader of the new article a better idea of the points you were addressing. By including the *entire* article, you'll only annoy those reading it. Also, signatures in the original aren't necessary; the readers already know who wrote it (by the attribution).

Avoid being tedious with responses—rather than pick apart an article, address it in parts or as a whole.

2. But not changing their words along the way, of course.

Addressing practically each and every word in an article only proves that the person responding has absolutely nothing better to do with his time.

If a "war" starts (insults and personal comments get thrown back and forth), *take it into email*—exchange email with the person you're arguing with. No one enjoys watching people bicker incessantly.

Crossposting The 'Newsgroups:' line isn't limited to just one group—an article can be posted in a list of groups. For instance, the line

```
Newsgroups: sci.space,comp.simulation
```

posts the article to both `sci.space` and `comp.simula-tion`. It's usually safe to cross-post to up to three or four groups. To list more than that is considered "excessive noise."

It's also suggested that if an article is cross-posted, a 'Followup-To:' header should be included. It should name the group to which all additional discussion should be directed. For the above example, a possible 'Followup-To:' would be

```
Followup-To: sci.space
```

which would make all follow-ups automatically posted to just `sci.space`, rather than to both `sci.space` and `comp.simulation`. If every response made with a news-reader's "followup" command should go to the person posting the article no matter what, there's also a mecha-nism worked in to accommodate this. The 'Followup-To:' header should contain the single word "poster":

```
Followup-To: poster
```

Certain newsreaders will use this to sense that a reply should never be posted back onto the Net. This is often used with questions that will yield a summary of information later, a vote, or an advertisement.

A Dying Boy's Last Wish

At least once every two to three months someone reposts a request from a dying boy, Craig, whose only desire is to get into the *Guinness Book of World Records* as having received the most postcards in history.

Over 33 million postcards were received by May 1991, and they continued to pour in. Craig achieved his goal, and was in the 1992 U.S. edition (look on page 207 of that copy); Guinness was so bothered by the volume of the response from the world community that they have discontinued the category. Craig is also fine—he was flown to Las Vegas by a generous businessman and treated by specialists.

As the Usenet Frequently Asked Questions list suggests, send the cost of postage to a worthy cause like UNICEF or the International Red Cross instead. There are many, many dying children who are just as needful of your support as Craig was.

Recent News

One should avoid posting recent events—sports scores, a plane crash, or whatever people will see on the evening news or read in the morning paper. By the time the article has propagated across all of Usenet, the news value of the article will have become stale. (This is one case for the argument that "Usenet news" is a misnomer.[3])

Computer Religion

No matter what kind of computer a person is using, it is always the *best* and most efficient of them all. Post-

3. Note that the ClariNet e.News service (see page 113) offers news items in a Usenet format as a precise *alternative* to the morning paper

ing articles asking questions like `"What computer should I buy? An Atari ST or an Amiga?"` will lead only to fervent arguments over the merits and drawbacks of each brand. Don't even ask the Net—go to a local user group or do some research of your own like reading some magazine reviews. Trying to say that one computer is somehow better than another is a moot point.

If you really need to make a point, write to a group called `alt.religion.computers` started by Bill Wisner of the University of Alaska. There, you can feel free to expound upon the virtues of your favorite computer manufacturer, operating system, or any other facet you deem worthy.

Quality of Postings

How you write and present yourself in your articles is important. If you have terrible spelling, keep a dictionary nearby. If you have trouble with grammar and punctuation, try to get a book on English grammar and composition (found in many bookstores and at garage sales). By all means pay attention to what you say—it makes you who you are on the Net.

Likewise, try to be clear in what you ask. Ambiguous or vague questions often lead to no response at all, leaving you, the poster, discouraged. Give as much essential information as you feel is necessary to let people help you but keep it within limits. For instance, you should probably include the operating system of your computer in the post if it's needed but don't tell everybody what peripherals you have.

*Useful
Subjects*

The '`Subject:`' line of an article is what will first attract people to read it—if it's vague or doesn't describe what's contained within, no one will read the article. At the same time, '`Subject:`' lines that are too wordy tend to be irritating. For example:

GOOD

Subject: Building Emacs on a Sun Sparc under 4.1

Subject: Tryin' to find Waldo in NJ.

BAD

Subject: I can't get Emacs to work!!!

Subject: I'm desperately in search of the honorable Mr. Waldo in the state of. . .

Simply put, try to think of what will best help the reader when he or she encounters your article in a newsreading session.

*Tone of
Voice*

Since common computers can't portray the inflection or tone in a person's voice, how articles are worded can directly affect the response to them. Suppose a discussion about older computing technology were going on; if you posted an article containing the remark

```
Anybody using a Vic-20 should go buy themselves
a life.
```

you'd definitely get some responses—telling you to take a leap. Rather than being inflammatory, phrase your articles in a way that rationally expresses your opinion, like

```
What're the practical uses of a Vic-20 these
days?
```

which presents you as a much more level-headed individual.

Also, what case (upper or lower) you use can indicate how you're trying to speak—netiquette dictates that if you USE ALL CAPITAL LETTERS, people will think you're "shouting." Write as you would in a normal letter to a friend, following traditional rules of English (or whatever language you happen to speak).

Frequently Asked Questions

A number of groups have a *Frequently Asked Questions* (FAQ) list, which gives the answers to questions or points that have been raised time and time again. FAQs are intended to help cut down redundant traffic. For example, in the group `alt.tv.simpsons,` one recurring question is, "Did you notice that there's a different blackboard opening at the beginning of every Simpsons episode?" As a result, it's part of the FAQ for that group.

Usually, FAQ lists are posted at the beginning of each month and set to expire one month later (when, supposedly, the next FAQ will be published). Nearly every FAQ is also crossposted to `news.answers,` which is used as a Usenet repository for them.

The RTFM Archive

In 1991, Jonathan Kamens, then of MIT, graciously set up a machine dedicated to the archiving and storage of the many periodic postings that are peppered throughout the various Usenet groups. Since he left, the staff at MIT has continued to maintain this service. To access the archive, FTP to the system `rtfm.mit.edu` and look in the directory '`/pub/usenet`'.

A Final Note

Before we go on, one thing must be pointed out. Usenet is a vast and complex thing. There are many things to learn about it. It is *not*, however, the major use of networks; by far, it's only a drop in the bucket compared to the whole of what can be done with this medium. Many fascinating things are being created around the world that are deserving of your attention—don't bury yourself in news.

"Be it true or false, so it be news."
— Ben Jonson, *News from the New World*

5 TELNET

T*elnet* is the main Internet protocol for creating an interactive connection with a remote machine. It gives the user the opportunity to be on one computer system and do work on another, which may be across the street or thousands of miles away. Distance no longer dictates the costs involved in creating connections—your organization (or you personally) most likely pay a set monthly fee for connectivity, regardless of what systems you communicate with. The ability to work with colleagues from around the world, explore the Net, and travel throughout Cyberspace, all from the comfort of your own office, home, or school, offers an unparalleled opportunity for discovery.

Using Telnet

As with FTP (see Chapter 3, *Anonymous FTP*), the actual command for negotiating a telnet connection varies from system to system. The most common is 'telnet' itself. It takes the form of:

59

`telnet` *somewhere.domain*

To be safe, we'll use your local system as a working example. By now, you hopefully know your site's FQDN. If not, *ask* or try to figure it out. You won't get by without it.

To open the connection, type

`telnet` *your.system.name*

If the system were `wubba.cs.widener.edu`, for example, the command would look like

`telnet wubba.cs.widener.edu`

The system will respond with something similar to

```
Trying 147.31.254.999...
Connected to wubba.cs.widener.edu.
Escape character is '^]'.
```

The escape *character*, in this example '`^]`' (hold down Control and type a right bracket), is the character that will let you go back to the local system to close the connection, suspend it, etc. To close this connection, you would type '`^]`', then respond to the `telnet>` prompt with the command `close`. Local documentation should be checked for information on specific commands, functions, and the escape character that can be used.

Telnet Ports   Many telnet clients also include a second option, the *port* on which the connection should take place. Normally, port 23 is the default telnet port; the user never has to think about it. But sometimes it's desirable to telnet to a different port on a system, where there may be a service available or to aid in debugging a problem. Using

```
telnet somewhere.domain port
```

will allow the user to connect to the given *port* on the system *somewhere.domain*. Again, this syntax is only approximate (some systems may use the command '`tel-net` *somewhere.domain*/`PORT`=*port*') and will vary from one operating system to another.

Many libraries use this port method to offer their facilities to the general Internet community; other services are also available. For instance, one would type

```
telnet martini.eecs.umich.edu 3000
```

to connect to the geographic server at the University of Michigan (see page 69). Other such port connections follow the same usage.

Publicly Accessible Libraries

Over the last several years, most university libraries have switched from a manual (card) catalog system to computerized library catalogs. The automated systems provide users with easily accessible and up-to-date information about the books available in these libraries. This has been further improved upon with the advent of local area networks, dial-up modems, and wide area networks (WANs). Now many of us can check on our local library's holdings or those of a library halfway around the world!

Many, many institutions of higher learning have made their library catalogs available for searching by anyone on the Internet. They include Boston University, the Colorado Alliance of Research Libraries (CARL), and London University King's College.

To include a listing of some of the existing sites would not only be far too long for this document, it would soon be out-of-date. Instead, several lists are being maintained and are available either by mail or via FTP. Also, the InterNIC *Directory of Directories* also describes the libraries that are accessible (see page 154 for further information).

Art St. George and Ron Larsen are maintaining a list of Internet-accessible libraries and databases often referred to as "the St. George directory." It began with only library catalogs but has expanded to include sections on other resources, from campus-wide information systems to bulletin-board systems that are not on the Internet. The library catalog sections are divided into those that are free, those that charge, and international (i.e., non-U.S.) catalogs; within each section they are arranged by state, province, or country. There is also a section giving dial-up information for some of the library catalogs. It's available for FTP (see Chapter 3, *Anonymous FTP*) on `nic.cerf.net` in the directory '`cerfnet/cerfnet_info/library_catalog`'. The file '`internetcatalogs`' has a date suffix; check for the most current date. The information is updated periodically.

For announcements of new libraries and discussion on related topics, consult the Usenet newsgroup `comp.internet.library`. (See Chapter 4, *Usenet News*, to learn about Usenet.)

Internet Services List

An invaluable resource is the *Internet Services List* maintained by Scott Yanoff of the University of Wisconsin at Milwaukee. Available via anonymous FTP from `ftp.csd.uwm.edu` in the directory '`/pub`' as '`inet.services.txt`', Scott's list incorporates the latest information regarding services offered over the Internet. Updates tend to come once every couple of weeks; they are also posted to the Usenet newsgroup `alt.internet.services`. A lot of the work that went into the rest of this chapter is derived from Scott's own achievements.

HYTELNET

Peter Scott of the University of Saskatchewan Library Systems Department created a remarkably useful program called *HYTELNET*; it provides a front end to accessing the Internet's many offerings. Every system mentioned in this chapter, plus many others, are reachable through HYTELNET's easy-to-use screen interface. Librarians have found the program particularly useful for searching library holdings halfway around the world without paying exorbitant communications fees.

Rather than have you try to remember the procedure for each available system, HYTELNET maintains a database of the necessary details for you, providing the information needed when you decide to explore a given database, library, or other resource. It combines the knowledge of all of the previously mentioned library and service lists into a cohesive and comprehensive system. In early 1992, HYTELNET was awarded the "Research and Education Networking Application Award" by Meckler Publishing.

The directory '`/pub/hytelnet`' on `ftp.usask.ca` houses the source code for the system—contact your system administrator about having it installed on your local system. The program originally supported the IBM PC and compatibles; support for Unix and VMS was added by Earl Fogel.

To be notified of updates to HYTELNET, you will need to join the 'LIB_HYTELNET' mailing list; contact Peter at scott@sklib.usask.ca to be added. He can be reached conventionally at:

Peter Scott
Systems Department
Univ. of Saskatchewan Libraries
Saskatoon, Saskatchewan, Canada S7N OWO
(306) 966-6014

The Cleveland Freenet

Freenets are open-access, free, community computer systems. One such system is the Cleveland Freenet, sponsored by CWRU (Case Western Reserve University). Anyone and everyone is welcome to join and take part in the exciting project—that of a National Telecomputing Public Network, where everyone benefits. There's *no* charge for the registration process and no charge to use the system.

To register on Freenet, telnet to any one of

```
freenet-in-a.cwru.edu
freenet-in-b.cwru.edu
freenet-in-c.cwru.edu
```

After you're connected, choose the entry on the menu that signifies you're a guest user. Another menu will follow; select 'Apply for an account', and you'll be well on your way to being a FreeNet member.

You will need to fill out a form and send it to them through the postal service—your login ID and password will be created in a short period of time. At that point you're free to use the system as you wish. They provide multiuser chat, email, Usenet news, and a variety of other things to keep you occupied for hours on end.

Directories

There are a few systems that are maintained to provide the Internet community with access to lists of information—users, organizations, etc. They range from fully dedicated computers with access to papers and research results to a system to find out about the faculty members of a university.

Knowbot   Knowbot is a "master directory" that contains email address information from the NIC WHOIS database (see page 107), the PSI White Pages Pilot Project, the NYSERNET X.500 database, and MCI Mail. Most of these services are email registries themselves, but Knowbot provides a very comfortable way to access all of them in one place. Telnet to `info.cnri.reston.va.us` on port 185.

White Pages   PSI maintains a directory of information on individuals. It will list the person's name, organization, and email address if it is given. Telnet to `wp.psi.net` and log in as '`fred`'. The White Pages Project also includes an interface to use X Windows remotely.

Databases and Other Resources

For information on database services, see page 113. Not all databases on the Internet require payment for use, though. There do exist some, largely research-driven, databases that are publicly accessible. New ones spring up regularly.

To find out more about the databases in this section, contact the people directly responsible for them. Their areas of concentration and the software used to implement them are widely disparate. Also, don't forget to check with your local library—the reference librarian there can provide information on conventional resources and, possibly, even those available over the Internet (they are becoming more common).

ATI-Net　　　　The Advanced Technology Information Network (ATI-Net) offers a collection of information about a variety of trade market issues. Among others, it includes general agricultural information and the Automated Trade Library Service, which provides, among other things, the ability to check current foreign exchange rates. (For example, if you're going to visit Ireland soon, you can find out what the exchange is between a US dollar and an Irish pound before you go to the bank for the currency.) Telnet to `caticsuf.cati.csufresno.edu` and log in with the username 'super'. You'll go through a relatively easy registration process to be able to use the system. For more information, contact:

Advanced Technology Information Network
(ATI-Net)
California State University, Fresno
2910 East Barstow Avenue
Fresno, CA 93740-0115 USA
`atimgr@cati.csufresno.edu`
(209) 278-4872
(209) 278-4849 (Fax)

AMS E-Math　　The American Mathematical Society (AMS) maintains a system for members of the AMS to learn about professional opportunities and new software. In addition, information on submitting reviews to *Mathematical Reviews* can be obtained by providing the system with your email address, and author lookups of people who have been published in the journal can be performed. Telnet to `e-math.ams.org` and log in with the username and password '`e-math`'. The files used to produce the *Bulletin of the AMS* are available on E-Math for download or reading.

Colorado Alliance of Research Libraries (CARL)

The Colorado Alliance of Research Libraries (CARL), in association with CARL Systems, Inc., operates a public-access catalog of services. Offered are a number of library databases, including searches for government periodicals, book reviews, indices for current articles, and access to other library databases around the country. Other services are available only to CARL members, including an online encyclopedia and their UnCover database, which describes thousands of journals and their contents. Telnet to `pac.carl.org` and log in as '`PAC`', or write to `help@carl.org` for more details.

Dartmouth Dante Project

Dartmouth College, in cooperation with Princeton University and the Dante Society of America, offers a unique service to literary scholars—the Dartmouth Dante Project. Telnet to `library.dartmouth.edu`; at the prompt type '`connect dante`'. The full text of Dante's *The Divine Comedy* (*La Commedia*), with over 600 years of commentary, can be examined by using a sophisticated search engine. The system can be queried by a given term or terms or by line—all references to a specified cantica (Inferno, Purgatorio, or Paradiso), canto, and line number will be returned. If you like, you can limit the results to a certain language (e.g., English, Latin, or Italian).

*European
Commission
Host
Organization
(ECHO)*

In 1980, the European Commission Host Organization (ECHO) was set up to demonstrate the benefits of using electronic information in the business world. The wide variety of databases—sporting more than 20 different areas of concentration—are available in all of the languages of the European Community. Among the topics covered are user guidance, scientific and R & D databases, industry and economy, and the language industry. In addition, the *I'M Guide* database contains the details of electronic information products and services available in Europe.

To access the ECHO system, telnet to `echo.lu` and enter 'ECHO' at the initial prompt. After choosing your preferred language (English, French, Spanish, etc.), you will be given a menu of the available databases and services. If you have any questions that are not answered by the online information, you can send mail to `echo@echo.lu`.

*NASA/IPAC
Extragalactic
Database*

The NASA/IPAC Extragalactic Database (NED) is an ongoing project, funded by NASA, to make data and literature on astronomical objects not belonging to our Milky Way galaxy available over computer networks. NED is an object-oriented database that contains extensive information, taken from major catalogs of galaxies, quasars, and infrared and radio sources, for over 200,000 extragalactic objects. NED provides positions, names, and other basic data (e.g., magnitude types, sizes, and redshifts) as well as bibliographic references and abstracts. Searches can be done by name, around a name, and by IAU shorthand. Search results can also be electronically mailed to the user. A tutorial is available that will guide a user through the retrieval process. Telnet to `ned.ipac.caltech.edu` and log in as 'ned'.

Clemson University Forestry and Agricultural Network

Clemson maintains a database similar to PENpages in content, but the information provided tends to be localized to the Southeastern United States. A menu-driven database offers queries involving weather, food, family, and human resources. Telnet to `eureka.clemson.edu` and log in as 'PUBLIC'. You need to be on a good VT100 emulator (or a real VT terminal).

Geographic Name Server

A geographic database listing information for cities in the United States and some international locations is maintained by Tom Libert (`libert@citi.umich.edu`). The database is searchable by city name, zip code, etc. It will respond with a lot of information: The area code, elevation, time zone, and longitude and latitude are included. For example, a query of "`04358`" yields

```
0 South China
1 23011 Kennebec
2 ME Maine
3 US United States
A 207
F 45 Populated place
L 44 23 44 N   69 34 18 W
E 223
Z 04358
```

To use the server, telnet to `geoserver.eecs.umich.edu` on port 3000. The command `help` will yield further instructions, along with an explanation for each of the fields in a response.

Ham Radio Callbook

A call-sign server was set up at the University at Buffalo by Devon Bowen, KA2NRC, to allow ham operators with Internet access to quickly find other hams without having to spend hours flipping through a paper callbook. The server, reached on port 2000 of `callsign.cs.buffalo.edu`, currently allows search by call sign, last name, city, or zip code. For information about the commands for the server, type `help`.

The database for the server is based on the FCC (U.S.) tapes acquired by Rusty Carruth, N7IKQ, and a DOC (Canada) database obtained by Alan Paeth, VE3AWP, WA3YOK. The U.S. portion of the database has no clubs.

If you're interested in contributing to maintaining the database, contact Devon Bowen, KA2NRC, either electronically at the email address `bowen@cs.buffalo.edu` or by regular postal mail to:

> Devon Bowen
> c/o Ken Smith
> Department of Computer Science
> State University of New York at Buffalo
> Buffalo, NY 14260 USA

The present maintainers accept donations of data from any country and in any format to help keep the server available. Monetary contributions can be in the form of sending purchased data to them at the above address.

LawNet

The Columbia University Law School computer center runs LawNet, a resource for lawyers and legal researchers alike. You have access to the Columbia online law library Pegasus, full text searching of information on law firms, the U.S. courts, and other material, and a gateway into HYTELNET. Telnet to `lawnet.law.columbia.edu` and log in as '`lawnet`'. If you have any trouble connecting to the library, write to their support staff at `culawcc@lawmail.law.columbia.edu`.

Library of
Congress

The Library of Congress in the United States has made a wealth of information available electronically. Their system, named LOCIS (the Library of Congress Information System), offers access to the entire Library of Congress catalog, information about federal legislation, searches on copyrights, and information about resources available from the Library of Congress for the blind and the deaf. Telnet to `locis.loc.gov`; type `help` to learn how to use the different ways you can search their databases.

NASA
SpaceLink

The Marshall Space Flight Center in Huntsville, Alabama, operates the NASA SpaceLink, a space-related informational database. Information on aeronautics, NASA news, NASA educational services, and the International Space Year (enacted by Congress to be 1992, the 500th anniversary of Columbus' birthday) can be examined. Telnet to `spacelink.msfc.nasa.gov` and log in with '`guest`' as the username; you won't be asked for a password. At any menu, type `?` to request additional information.

Net Mail Sites

Merit, Inc., provides a Net Mail Sites database to aid people in the search for a given university, company, or other network party. It maintains a database with Internet, UUCP, and BITNET host listings. Telnet to `hermes.merit.edu` and enter '`netmailsites`' at main prompt. The system will ask you to enter the name of a site to search for and will respond with the mail information for each of the three major networks. Searching for "swarthmore," for example, yields:

```
:Enter the name of a site -> swarthmore

There are 3 sites found for SWARTHMORE
```

```
Internet Sites:
  CAMPUS.SWARTHMORE.EDU


Bitnet Sites:
  SWATPRM    Swarthmore College Computing Center - VAX


UUCP Sites:
  swatsun    Swarthmore College Computer Science Dept.
```

Some of the information for the Internet will be incomplete (e.g., searching for "widener" yields Widener University's old BITNET name and present UUCP name but not any of its Internet names); nonetheless, using Net Mail Sites is an excellent tool for finding addresses.

Ocean Network Information Center

The University of Delaware College of Marine Studies offers access to an interactive database of research information covering all aspects of marine studies, nicknamed OCEANIC. This includes the World Oceanic Circulation Experiment (WOCE) information and program information, research ship schedules and information, and a Who's Who of email and mailing addresses for oceanic studies. Data from a variety of academic institutions based on research studies is also available. Telnet to `delocn.udel.edu` and log in as 'INFO'.

PENpages

PENpages is an agriculturally oriented database administered by Pennsylvania State University. Information entered into PENpages is provided by a number of sources, including the Pennsylvania Dept. of Agriculture, Rutgers University, and Penn State. Easy-to-use menus guide users to information ranging from cattle and agricultural prices to current weather information, from health information to agricultural news from around the nation. A keyword search option also allows users to search the database for related information and articles. The database is updated daily, and a listing of most recent additions is displayed after login. Telnet to `psupen.psu.edu` and log in as the user 'PNOTPA'.

Science and Technology Information System

The STIS is maintained by the National Science Foundation (NSF) and provides access to many NSF publications. The full text of publications can be searched online and copied from the system, which can accommodate up to ten users at one time. Telnet to `stis.nsf.gov` and log in as 'public'. Everything on the system is also available via anonymous FTP. For further information, contact:

STIS, Office of Information Resource
   Management
National Science Foundation
4201 Wilson Blvd., Room 245
Arlington, VA 22230 USA
`stis@nsf.gov`
(703) 306-1129
(703) 306-0201 (Fax)

SuperNet

Advanced Networks & Services, Inc., maintains "SuperNet," an information search service. It offers a news service, information on the Internet (glossaries, RFCs, etc.), a Job Bank listing positions at business and academic institutions throughout the United States and overseas, newsletters such as *Vector Register* and *Dataquest Perspective*, and maintains six months of back issues of *Supercomputing Review* magazine—the latest volume is available at the end of each month. Telnet to `supernet.ans.net` and log in as '`supernet`'.

Washington University Services

Washington University maintains a user-friendly gateway to many of the services listed in this section, along with many libraries and similar resources. You can choose a system to which to automatically connect by selecting from a well-organized menu of choices. Telnet to `library.wustl.edu` and just press Return at the '`Username:`' prompt.

Weather Services

The University of Michigan's Department of Atmospheric, Oceanic, and Space Sciences maintains a database of weather and related information for the United States and Canada. Available are current weather conditions and forecasts for cities in the U.S. and Canada, a national weather summary, ski conditions, earthquake and hurricane updates, and a listing of severe weather conditions. Telnet to `downwind.sprl.umich.edu` on port 3000 to use the system.

The Atmospheric Science and Environmental Program at the University of Alabama at Huntsville also runs a weather server; telnet to `wind.atmos.uah.edu` on port 3000.

Bulletin Board Systems

There are a number of bulletin-board systems (BBSes) available on the Internet. Some are "traditional"— they're there for people to use to confer, have an interactive chat, and read local news announcements. Others were started for organizations to make information available to the general public, both through regular modem dial-up and over the Internet.

▸ *Air Pollution*

The United States Environmental Protection Agency runs a BBS with information about air pollution, their policies, and other useful facts. Telnet to `ttnbbs.rtpnc.epa.gov`; after you've connected, press the Return key once to start the session.

▸ *American Philosophical Association*

The APA bulletin board includes information on the organization's regular proceedings, notices about grants, fellowships, and jobs; APA members can send questions to the national office and submit short items for inclusion on the board. Telnet to `eis.calstate.edu` and log in as 'bbs'.

▸ *Denver University*

In Colorado, Denver University has made available a bulletin board that offers its users email, Usenet news, and many other treats. You must have a notary public certify your registration, because the system was severely abused in its early days. Telnet to `nyx.cs.du.edu` and log in as 'new'.

▸ *Food and Drug Administration*

The United States Food and Drug Administration started a bulletin board to make information about their policies, recent decisions, and regulations available to the public. Telnet to `fdabbs.fda.gov` and log in as 'bbs'.

▸ *Newton*

A BBS for people teaching or studying science, math, or computer science is run by the Argonne National Laboratory in Argonne, Illinois. Telnet to `newton.dep.anl.gov` and log in as 'bbs'.

▶ *Rutgers University*

The Quartz BBS at Rutgers has been one of the longest-lasting among Internet bulletin boards. It is often busy but will give you pointers to other systems you can try in the meantime. Telnet to `quartz.rutgers.edu` and log in as 'bbs'.

▶ *UNC at Chapel Hill*

The University of North Carolina operates a very successful Internet BBS on `launchpad.unc.edu`; log in as 'launch'.

▶ *University of Iowa*

A popular BBS, called ISCA, is run at the University of Iowa. Telnet to `bbs.isca.uiowa.edu` and log in as 'guest'.

Information about new bulletin boards is often posted to the newsgroup `alt.bbs.internet`. Also, Scott Yanoff's list (see page 62) includes many BBSes in its collection of things you can try.

"My consciousness suddenly switched locations, for the first time in my life, from the vicinity of my head and body to a point about twenty feet away from where I normally see the world."
— Howard Rheingold, *Virtual Reality*

6 WWW: WORLD WIDE WEB

$\mathbf{O}$ne of the chief complaints about the Internet is that it's too difficult to use for those who aren't very comfortable with technical information. As an approach to answering this problem, efforts were made to incorporate the idea of *hypertext*—cross-referencing information by just having to "point and click" on one item to go to another—into a more friendly interface to the Internet. The end result of this work is what many people now use as their introduction to Cyberspace: the World Wide Web.

Commonly referred to as "the Web" or by its acronym *WWW*, the World Wide Web is fast becoming the largest source of network traffic around the world. Even online services like America Online, Prodigy, and CompuServe have joined in the fray, providing Web browsing tools for their subscribers. This allows these customers to take full advantage of the Internet while on the systems to which they've already become accustomed. Other regional and national services provide packages that invariably include interfaces to the Web; in fact, the presence of these tools has in a very short length of time become the de facto standard among the expectations of online users.

The Beginning

If ever anyone has doubted the short length of time that the Internet has been in general use, the Web is a prime example of how quickly things can change. In early 1993, the World Wide Web was a project that had only a modicum of public visibility outside the highly specialized technical interest. A year later, it had become far more popular and was gaining public notice in newspapers around the world. And in 1995, it could be found mentioned repeatedly on television, included as a point of contact in the advertisements of magazines like *Rolling Stone*, and actively used in elementary schools for educational tools like staying up-to-date on the exploration of the Arctic Ocean.

Using the Web

Web pages are written in *HTML*, the HyperText Markup Language. The raw text—the actual HTML "code"—is directly transmitted to the Web browser, which in turn displays the information in a controlled, deliberate form. This makes it possible to offer the graphic display of its contents based on the offerings of the system being used or even do proper output on a text-only screen.

Web Browsers

To take advantage of the information presented on the Web, you will use a tool called a Web *browser*. There are a variety of these available either commercially or, more commonly, for free via anonymous FTP.[1] In addition, many online services now include a browser as a part of their own software. The choices include Mosaic—the first Web browser made available for general use—as well as Netscape, Lynx, NetCruiser, WebExplorer, and many others. While they are available for Unix systems, the Web is most frequently browsed by using software on PCs and Macintosh computers.

You will start the Web browser by either typing its name at the command line (e.g., 'mosaic' or 'netscape'), or clicking on its icon. Once the program has started, it will connect to a "default" Web page that it uses as an initial point of reference. Most Web browsers can be configured to refer to a particular Web site at startup, most commonly a local Web page. To exit from graphic browsers, you will usually choose a 'File' pull-down menu and choose the last entry, often 'Exit' or 'Quit'.

URLs

The Uniform Resource Locator, or *URL*, is the centerpiece of navigating the Web. In a fairly compact and succinct format, the URL allows users to point directly to the Web site or, more importantly, the exact Web page that is of interest. While browsing the Web, you will discover that your ability to think of sites in terms of their URLs will become easier over time. Don't become discouraged if you find it difficult to remember the apparently obscure format of a URL—after you've referenced them for a month or so, it will slowly make more sense.

The basic format of a URL is:

```
http://somewhere.com/item
```

The first portion, "http://", is unchanging for most

---

1. See Chapter 3, *Anonymous FTP*, to learn how to transfer files with FTP.

URLs. That is followed by the site name and a trailing slash, like "`http://www.eff.org/`". It may be followed by further information (the *item* noted above), to point the browser at a specific Web page or item—e.g., a specific graphics file. However, you can start browsing a particular Web site without this information. For example, to browse the Web site that contains my Web page, you could use the URL `http://www.zen.org/`.

The *item* field can point to a specific file, a directory (if the *item* named is followed by a trailing slash), or other choices. Thus, referring to the URL '`http://www.geo.ed.ac.uk/quakes/quakes.html`' asks the server for the file '`quakes.html`'. Using a trailing slash implies a request for the file '`index.html`' in that directory. If there is no such file there, a request for the URL `http://www.xmission.com/~arts/` would bring up a raw listing of the directory '`art`'.

As you can see, a URL is a single line of information with a uniform structure to it. In the beginning of this chapter, you read how many magazines and commercials refer to a URL for their particular company or product. In addition, you will sometimes come across a business card that not only lists the person's mailing address and phone number but also an email address and a Web page.

Home Pages   When you meet someone and the Internet comes up in conversation (yes, this can happen more often than one might expect—or even like), you may be asked for the URL to your *home page*. This is the more common term used to describe a personal Web page. The information on home pages can include anything, ranging from a picture to a description of hobbies and interests to a list of personel favorite Web pages (items on their *hotlist*).

The creativity used in setting up a home page has become something of a competition. People who may not normally use extensive imagination with art or writing will find themselves compelled to take great pride in their handiwork. This pride is also exhibited in being able to say that yes, you do have a home page, and that you know the URL without having to look it up.

However, it's recommended that readers get a good feel for the general offerings of the Web before they take on this task. If you cannot resist the urge, it may be helpful to seek advice on possible approaches to the page's layout from friends who have already written their own, .

Other Types of URLs   While the "`http://somewhere.com/`" heading is the most common format for a URL, there are some exceptions. They include:

• *FTP sites*   Many Web pages will refer to a particular directory or specific item available when using anonymous FTP. The URL that points the browser to these items is of the form `ftp://site.com/dir/filename`. Your Web software then performs an anonymous FTP connection and retrieves the file. For example, `ftp://ftp.cert.org/pub/01-README` will retrieve '`01-README`' from CERT's FTP site.

• *Alternate Ports*   Some servers run on an alternative to the "default" port for the Web connections. If you ever see a URL that has a number in it, as in `http://www.cs.cmu.edu:8001/Web/books.html`, it just means that the Web server for that particular item is running on port 8001 of the system. (Again, this is usually not something you'll need to worry about; just accept this kind of URL to be a standard one.)

• *Specific Sections*   Some Web pages are rather large in size, composed of a large amount of information. In order to point the browser at a specific section of the text, a URL can be appended with the name of a particular section. For example, a Web page will refer the browser to the URL when the display should skip ahead in 'hotlist.html' to the section tagged with the name 'music'.

• *Telnet sites*   A link that points to a particular site that you would log in to will refer to the URL telnet://*sitename.com*/ or, if a particular user login is to be used, telnet://*user@sitename.com*/. It then performs a telnet connection, as discussed in Chapter 5. For example, to log in to the On-Line Bookstore, one would point the Web browser at telnet://books.com/.

• *Program Arguments*   A form is often used by the user to provide specific criteria before sending in a query. When the server gets the URL for the request, it will look like:

```
http://www.zen.org/cgi-bin/search?recipe=chicken
```

The text from the question mark on is given to the program as a sequence of arguments, which can be used to produce a custom Web page with the results using those settings.

Basic Commands   Perhaps the most frequent option used with a Web browser is Open. This will prompt you for a particular URL to visit. If you make a mistake typing the name, the browser will tell you that it was unable to access that particular Web page.

However, the most common action is to actually click on a particular point of a Web page, to visit another. You will notice that some items on a page are either in another color, a bold face, have the words underlined, or have a border around them. If you click your mouse on that item or press Return if it's a text browser, you will follow that "link" to another URL. It may be another item at that site or be something offered by another system. For example, you may see

> If you're interested in literature, there's a page about **the work of William Shakespeare.**

If you click your mouse anywhere on the words "William Shakespeare," the browser will then visit a site with a collection of the master's works. That page will then also refer to others, carrying work of the similar genre, information about critical analysis of English literature, etc.

Another option of the browser that you will find yourself clicking on fairly often is 'Back.' It will move to the previous Web page that you visited. This is very useful when you're consulting a list of possible Web pages; you can move down the list, visiting each that is of interest. If you decide to choose another from the same list, you simply click on 'Back' to return to the page bearing the list. Some Web pages offer an item you can use to "move back" to its parent page; for example, the William Shakespeare Web page will include an arrow you can click on to move "back" to the page creator's home page. Don't get confused, though—that option won't necessarily move you back to the last page you were looking at.

If you want to stop receiving a Web page, simply click on the 'Stop' button. Sometimes you will begin to visit a particular page and realize either that it's not what you really wanted to do or that it carries with it a number of large images. If you are using a relatively "slow" Net connection, this can prove to be a test of your patience—just how long you're willing to wait to receive a full page. In those cases, you can click on `Stop` shortly after you know the browser is receiving the images, and still have a usable page displayed. Some Web browsers also allow you to avoid loading graphic images by choice. For example, the Netscape browser includes an option called "Auto Load Images," which requires the user to click on an `Images` button to download the graphics used on a Web page.

Finally, the `Reload` button will let you revisit the page you're currently reading. This can be handy when you're visiting a site that may have changed the information since you last read the page. Many browsers use a method called *caching* to speed up your Web travels; each time a page or image is transferred, the browser keeps a copy of it. That way, if you visit that site again, the browser will use the local files to present the majority of the page, rather than using up network bandwidth transferring the files repeatedly.

Types of Pages

The fundamental style used for a Web page is just plain text, with references (or "links") to other sites. However, there are a number of other techniques that can be used along with the plain text.

An *image map* presents a very user friendly interface to a collection of information. Rather than concentrate on words, a user will be given a graphic image with particular areas that will result in connection to another page. For example, Southwest Airlines has a very friendly image offering information about its flights at `http://www.iflyswa.com/`. If you click on the cash register, you can find out the costs of particular travel itineraries. Similarly, clicking on the telephone will bring up a page listing the phone numbers you can use to reach them.

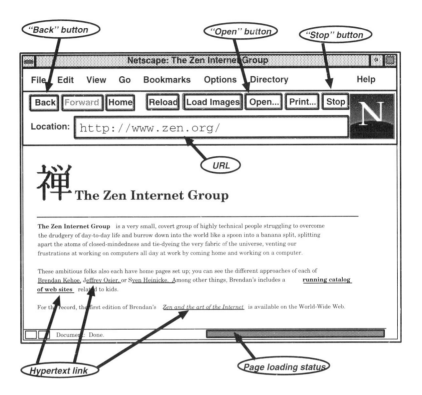

The same technology is used to present simulated "button" lists. Analogous to the point-and-click approach of modern computers, many Web pages offer a series of boxes that offer particular choices. For example, a list may include "Product Information," "What's New," and "Art Gallery." Clicking on the box containing the words of your choice will bring you to the connecting page—all offered in a more friendly, intuitive manner than highlighted text.

Forms are used to allow users to fill out particular criteria, then submit their request. For example, the sites that index the contents of Web pages around the world use a form interface to allow you to type the words you wish to find in your search.

Searching the Web

As the Web grew in popularity and new Web pages were being added in great numbers every day, the Web suffered one drawback that many Net services share: There was no organization to its offerings. The information was in seemingly random locations, with no concrete method of finding pages on a particular subject.

To address this need, a few sites began to run Web index services to make it possible to search for URLs' addressing. First created out of curiosity to see if such a service could be of use to the Net community, many grew to use very fast computers and were given commercial support to improve their overall performance.

The most popular services include

`http://www2.infoseek.com/`	*InfoSeek*
`http://lycos.cs.cmu.edu/`	*Lycos*
`http://webcrawler.com/`	*WebCrawler*
`http://www.yahoo.com/`	*Yahoo*

The first three services let you type one or more words and search their indices for matches of varying accuracy, ranging from matching just one of the words you gave to matching all of them. The fourth, Yahoo, is sorted by subject area (though word searches are possible) and went from a part-time project to a commercially sponsored Internet directory and search engine as a result of its popularity. If you're wondering if there's a Web page on a particular topic, Yahoo is the first place to look.

All four of the services listed also allow people to request to have their own Web pages included in the listings. The contents are updated regularly to help avoid references to cancelled pages.

If you are interested in doing searches in many databases on a commercial level, point your Web browser at the original InfoSeek URL of `http://www.infoseek.com/`. It offers subscriptions to the full level of service, allowing searches of thousands of newsgroups, half a million Web pages, wire services, movie reviews, and more. For more information about subscribing to InfoSeek, write to `info@infoseek.com`.

Web Pages

So where should you start? Following are some possible sites to visit that show some of the diversity of the Web. With the search engines described above and discoveries from the Web pages that you come across, you should be able to find online information in almost any particular area of interest.

If you'd rather not type in all of the URLs, visit

`http://www.zen.org/fourth/hotlist.html`

and you'll be able to click on each one individually.

The Louvre	`http://www.cnam.fr/louvre/`
BBC	`http://www.bbcnc.org.uk/tv/`
Online Dating	`http://www.match.com/`
Movie Reviews	`http://www.film.com/film/`
FBI Top Ten Most Wanted List	`http://conxtion.com/fbi/fbi.htm`

San Francisco Chronicle	`http://www.sfgate.com/chronicle/`
Newspapers Around the World	`http://www.nando.net/epage/htdocs/links/newspapers.html`
Play Black-Jack	`http://www.ua.com/blackjack/bj.html`
Travels with Samantha	`http://martigny.ai.mit.edu/samantha/travels-with-samantha.html`
Web Sites in Ireland	`http://slarti.ucd.ie/maps/ireland.html`
Online Books	`http://www.cs.cmu.edu:8001/Web/books.html`
The Electronic Zoo	`http://netvet.wustl.edu/e-zoo.htm`
Useless WWW Pages	`http://www.primus.com/staff/paulp/useless.html`
United States Postal Service	`http://www.usps.gov/`
Internet Underground Music Archive	`http://www.iuma.com/`
FedEx Shipping and Tracking	`http://www.fedex.com/`

HotWired Magazine	`http://www.hotwired.com/`
Send a Card over the Net	`http://infopages.com/card/`
Federal Information Exchange	`http://web.fie.com/`
AIDS Patents Project	`http://concord.cnidr.org/welcome.html`

"*'Tis true; there's magic in the web of it.*"
— William Shakespeare
Othello, act 3, scene 4

7 VARIOUS TOOLS

New and interesting ways to use the Internet are being dreamed up every day. As they gain widespread use, some methods become near-standard (or actual written-standard) Internet tools. A few are described in this chapter—there are undoubtedly others, and new ideas spring up all the time. An active user of the Internet will discover most of the more common ones in time. Usually, these services are free. See Chapter 8, *Commercial Services*, for applications that are commercially available over the Internet.

Usenet is often used to announce a new service or capability on the Internet. In particular, the groups `alt.internet.services` and `comp.internet.net-happenings` are good places to look. Information will drift into other areas as word spreads. Also, the InterNIC Info Scout (see page 129) will send you mail when new services and resources are announced.

Finger

On many systems there exists the `finger` command, which provides information about each user who's currently logged in. This command also has extensions for use over the Internet. Under normal circumstances, one would simply type `finger` for a summary of who's logged in to the local system, or `finger username` for specific information about a user.

It's also possible to go one step further and go onto the network:

```
finger @hostname
```

To see who is currently logged in on `zen.org`, for example, use

```
% finger @zen.org
[zen.org]
Login    Name           TTY Idle  When      Where
jeffrey  Jeffrey Osier  la        Sat  3:08
brendan  Brendan Kehoe  p1    13 Sat 14:44 zen:0.0
brendan  Brendan Kehoe  p2       Sat 14:44 zen:0.0
sven     Sven Heinicke  p3 1:14 Sat 12:23 get.wired.com
```

To find out about a certain user, the user can be fingered specifically (and need not be logged in):

```
% finger bart@cs.widener.edu
[cs.widener.edu]
Login name: bart                     In real life: Bart Simpson
Directory: /home/springfield/bart Shell: /bin underachieve
Affiliation: Brother of Lisa    Home System: channel29.fox.org
Last login Thu May 23 12:14 (EDT) on ttyp6 from channel29.fox.org.
No unread mail
Project: To become a ''fluff'' cartoon character.
Plan:
Don't have a cow, man.
```

Please realize that some sites are very security-conscious and need to restrict access to information about their systems and users. To that end, they often block `finger` requests from outside sites—so don't be surprised if fingering a computer or a user gives you the message "`Connection refused`".

There are a few systems that offer services by fingering a certain address. If you finger `weather@synoptic.mit.edu`, for example, you will find out if it's raining around MIT's Tech Square. The address `quake@geophys.washington.edu` will offer information on earthquakes and other seismic data. By fingering the address `nasanews@space.mit.edu`, you'll find out the latest in NASA Headline News. See page 129 for a description of a rather novel use of finger.

Ping

The `ping` command allows the user to check if another system is currently up and running. The general form of the command is `ping` *system* .[1] For example, typing

```
ping cs.widener.edu
```

will tell you if the main machine in Widener University's Computer Science lab is currently online. (They certainly hope so!)

Many implementations of `ping` also include an option to let you see how fast a link is running (to give you some idea of the load on the network).

---

1. The usage will, again, vary.

```
% ping -s cs.swarthmore.edu
PING cs.swarthmore.edu: 56 data bytes
64 bytes from 130.58.68.1: icmp_seq=0 ttl=251 time=66 ms
64 bytes from 130.58.68.1: icmp_seq=1 ttl=251 time=45 ms
64 bytes from 130.58.68.1: icmp_seq=2 ttl=251   time=46 ms
^C
--- cs.swarthmore.edu ping statistics ---
3 packets transmitted, 3 packets received, 0% packet loss
round-trip min/avg/max = 45/52/66 ms
```

This case tells us that for cs.swarthmore.edu, it takes about 46 milliseconds for a packet to go from Widener to Swarthmore College and back again. It also gives the average and worst-case speeds and any packet loss that may have occurred (e.g., because of network congestion).

While ping generally doesn't hurt network performance, you shouldn't use it *too* often—usually once or twice will leave you relatively sure of the other system's state.

© 1995. Washington Post Writers Group. Reprinted with permission.

Talk

Sometimes email is clumsy and difficult to manage when one really needs to have an interactive conversation. The Internet provides for that as well, in the form of *talk*. Two users can literally see each other type across thousands of miles.

To talk with Bart Simpson at Widener, one would type

```
talk bart@cs.widener.edu
```

which would cause a message similar to the following to be displayed on Bart's terminal:

```
Message from Talk_Daemon@cs.widener.edu at 21:45 ...
talk: connection requested by joe@ee.someplace.edu
talk: respond with: talk joe@ee.someplace.edu
```

Bart would, presumably, type '`talk joe@ee.someplace.edu`' to answer your request. You could then chat about whatever you wished, with instantaneous response time, rather than the write-and-wait style of email. To leave `talk`, on many systems one would type `Ctrl-C` (hold down the Control key and press 'c'). Check a local manual to be sure.

There are two different versions of talk in common use today. The first, dubbed "old talk," is used by systems whose software hasn't been updated or revised in a while. The second, `ntalk` (aka "new talk"), is more the standard. If, when attempting to talk with another user, the system responds with an error about protocol families, odds are the incompatibilities between versions of talk is the culprit. It's up to the system administrators of sites that use the old talk to install `ntalk` for their users.

Internet Relay Chat (IRC)

Many online services include *chat* areas. Split up into virtual "rooms," these areas allow groups of people to talk about a particular topic or, in most cases, just hold a general conversation. The one drawback of this form of communication on these services is the fact that they are commercially driven: You will need to pay for the time you spend using them.

The Internet Relay Chat, or *IRC*, is the Internet's free equivalent to this service. While the `talk` command allows one person to talk directly with another, IRC offers the ability to have many people talk together.

Started in 1988, IRC has become a popular activity around the world. By simply running a local program, you're able to talk to large groups of people at any time, day or night.

To use IRC, the command you'll probably type on your local system is `irc`. This will connect you to a particular server, chosen by your system administrator when installing the software.[2] After you connect with the server, you will have a number of possible options;

typing the command /help will provide a list of the different instructions that the program will accept. Each of the commands begins with a leading slash ('/'), to distinguish it from a line to be transmitted. You won't need to know about very many of the commands to use IRC.

While you're talking, you'll be using a *nickname*. Your IRC program will give you one by default; to change it, you can type the command /NICK newname, telling it to attribute what you wrote to *newname*. If you choose the nickname 'jsteam', your messages will appear as:

```
<jsteam> hi jessie! where are you from?
```

Given the number of people who use IRC at a given moment, there's a strong likelihood that your choice for a nickname will have already been taken. In this case, you can try a small variation on it or try others until you finally pick one that isn't in use.

A *channel* is the term used for a particular chat area under IRC. To list the channels that are currently available, type /list. Be prepared—there will often be more channels than you can begin to choose from. To reduce the number of channels listed, try typing the command

```
/list -min 25
```

This will name only those channels with 25 or more people on them. (As you can see, the options used in IRC are not necessarily intuitive; read the online help before you start experimenting.) In response, the program will print lines of the form:

2. IRC software is available via anonymous FTP from cs-ftp.bu.edu in the directory '/irc'.

```
*** #newchat 28 Welcome to Newchat..... The Friendliest Channel On IRC
```

Thus the channel '`#newchat`' is shown to currently have 28 people using it. The name of each channel has a pound sign as its first character.

To enter a channel, type the command `/join #channel`, where *channel* is the name of the one you wish to visit. The most common area that people will join when using IRC for the first time is '`#newchat`', one of the names we saw listed earlier. To talk with other people who are also trying to get used to IRC, you would type `/join #newchat`.

The moment you are told that you have joined the channel, you will immediately start seeing messages appear. It may take a few moments to get a feel for how the conversation is flowing on a channel before you participate. The speed of IRC as a whole may shock you at first; as with many aspects of the Internet, you may expect messages to take a fair length of time to reach everyone else. Instead, you'll get replies from people only moments after you sent what you wrote.

To send a message, simply type the words you want to say and press the Return key. A few seconds later, you will see the message listed; this means that it's now being broadcast to all of the other people talking in that channel. There are a variety of ways that you can talk to people on a channel. For example, instead of just typing a plain text line, you can have IRC present your message as an "action." Rather than have a message appear as

```
<MaryL> I love going climbing in the mountains.
```

the user with the nickname "`MaryL`" can type her sentence with the command `/me` as the first characters in it.

This will make IRC send

```
* MaryL wishes she could go mountain climbing
```

This approach can make a discussion appear to have activity going on within it and make the channel even more entertaining.

If you want to change channels, use the `/join` command with the name of the new channel; you may want to get the list of channels before you move, since the one you're thinking of may have vanished.

Finally, to leave IRC completely you can type '`/quit`' at any time.

It should be noted that online chat systems, including IRC, definitely have their negative side. And unlike commercial services, IRC does not have any barriers. Systems like America Online and Prodigy hire people to monitor public talks, with the aim of avoiding abusive or dangerous discussions. IRC, on the other hand, is completely open. Parents will want to be very careful before allowing their children to use IRC unmonitored.

While occasionally attractive, a chat system can cause people to become addicted—letting everyday life yield to time spent in a virtual community where everyone is equal, and unseen.

Talking with others online is an excellent way for people with disabilities of one form or another (physical, speech, etc.) to interact at a level that is often difficult in real life. It also provides you with an outlet for frustration, curiosity, and an ability to present ideas to others in a safe setting. But keep in mind that this kind of communication is significantly limited in comparison to direct, face-to-face discussion. Keep yourself detached from your computer enough to stay in touch with reality.

Internet Navigation

When the Internet was still young, its creators faced a difficult challenge: how to make volumes of information available electronically. Finding space for all of the text, sound, and video that should be online was crucial. Since then, the price for storage has fallen dramatically. Also, the technology, in the form of optical character recognition (OCR) software, to convert printed text into electronic data is readily available to anyone who wants it.

As a direct result, there are now well over a billion bytes of raw information available for public consumption on the Internet. The issue has shifted from how to get all of the bits online to how to navigate through such a glut of information to find what is really needed.

Within a few months of each other, two new tools began to be used heavily on the Net. The first, the Wide Area Information Server (WAIS), lets you ask simple questions of a vast range of databases, covering all areas of interest from molecular biology to the Bible. The second, the Internet gopher, lets you walk your way through the Net, window-shopping, until you discover what you're looking for.

Wide Area Information Server (WAIS)

One of the most powerful tools to appear in recent years has been the Wide Area Information Server (WAIS) system. (WAIS is pronounced "ways.") Started as a collaborative project between Thinking Machines, Dow Jones/News Retrieval, and Apple

Computer, WAIS lets you search huge bodies of text in very little time.

The information in WAIS is divided into separate "sources"—there are well over 250 of them (so far), covering a wide range of topics. For example, you can search the King James version of the Bible for the phrase "burning bush," or look up synonyms for the word "travel" in a copy of *Roget's Thesaurus*.

There are a number of interfaces to WAIS—clients are available for the X Window System, NeXT systems, Macintoshes, and PCs. Similarly, there is a screen-based version (called `swais`) that lets you use WAIS on a normal terminal screen, rather than a fancy workstation. To try WAIS without using special local software, telnet to `quake.think.com` and log in as 'wais'. Each client (and the system you can telnet to) has online help to teach you what the keys and mouse selections will do.

The main idea behind WAIS is to let you search one or more of the sources for a given question (sometimes called a collection of keywords). If you ask WAIS the question "Tell me about DNA" and you select a few biology sources, you will likely get a number of *hits*, or matches, that include the information you were looking for. However, if you also select the source for movie reviews included with all of the other matches, you will probably end up with a review of the movie *Jurassic Park*.

Since a question can end up giving you a lot of information you probably didn't expect, the result of a query is rated on a scale from 1 to 1000. A "score" of 1000 means a particular hit has a high likelihood of being what you were looking for. Likewise, a low score—say, 283—probably means the information in that hit won't be too useful, but it's included anyway, in case you need it.

The mailing list `wais-discussion@think.com` is a periodic digest of messages about WAIS and similar issues; write to `wais-discussion-request@think.com` to subscribe. The list is also gatewayed into the Usenet newsgroup `comp.infosystems.wais`.

If you'd like to try the client software (your system administrator may need to install it for you), everything is available via anonymous FTP from the system `ftp.cnidr.org`.

The Internet Gopher

The students and staff of the University of Minnesota created a service called *gopher*, which lets you browse the Internet in a very comfortable and intuitive manner (burrowing your way under the Internet, to pop up where the information is, much like the cute and fuzzy gopher that keeps pestering your garden). Gopher makes it easy to access resources on the Internet in their many forms: as files to be transferred, services you telnet to, or WAIS databases you can search.

Since its first public introduction in December 1991, the total network traffic generated by gopher usage ballooned from 5 megabytes per month to over 100 gigabits per month in May of 1993. To put it another way, gopher really hit the ground running.

There are a number of ways to access gopher, ranging from a textbased interface for Unix, VMS, and DOS, to slick X Window and Macintosh windowed clients. All of this software is available on the site `boombox.micro.umn.edu` in the directory '`/pub/gopher`'. If you don't have a local gopher client (try typing the command `gopher` at your prompt), you can try it by telnetting to the system `consultant.micro.umn.edu` and logging in as '`gopher`'.

A typical gopher session presents you with an initial

menu of things to look under. The default gopher server for the text-based clients (the original one at the University of Minnesota) presents you with a number of selections:

```
        Internet Gopher Information Client v2.1.3
           Root gopher server: gopher.tc.umn.edu


-->1.   Information About Gopher/
   2.   Computer Information/
   3.   Discussion Groups/
   4.   Fun & Games/
   5.   Internet file server (ftp) sites/
   6.   Libraries/
   7.   News/
   8.   Other Gopher and Information Servers/
   9.   Phone Books/
  10.   Search Gopher Titles at the University of Minnesota <?>
  11.   Search lots of places at the University of Minnesota <?>
  12.   University of Minnesota Campus Information/


   Press ? for Help, q to Quit             Page: 1/1
```

If the initial gopher page that you see is not the one above—many sites have their own servers—you can use the command

```
gopher gopher.tc.umn.edu
```

to connect directly to the server used as the sample for this section.

Each entry in the list is of a specific type; for example, a trailing slash (/) at the end means that there is other information beneath an entry. The symbol '<TEL>' after an entry means it's something you will telnet to (gopher will tell you what account you need to log in with, if any), and '<?>' means it's something you can search, like a WAIS index or a database of movie reviews.

You press the Return key to move down into another area and use the 'u' key to move back up. In the previous menu, if you were to press Return on News, you'd see a new menu of things related to different kinds of news.

```
              Internet Gopher Information Client v2.1.3
                               News

-->1.    AMInews Ski Reports
    2.    Cornell Chronicle (Weekly)/
    3.    French Language Press Review/
    4.    IT Connection (University of Minnesota)
    5.    Minnesota Daily/
    6.    NASA News
    7.    National Weather Service Forecasts/
    8.    Other Newspapers, Magazines, and Newsletters /
    9.    Purdue University News
    10.   Technolog (Institute of Technology, University of Minnesota)/
    11.   The Bucknellian Student Newspaper at Bucknell University/
    12.   The Daily Illini (University of Illinois)/
    13.   The Gazette (University of Waterloo)/
    14.   The University of Chicago Chronicle (biweekly)/
    15.   USENET News (from Michigan State)/
    16.   University of Alabama at Birmingham Kaleidoscope/
    17.   University of Minnesota News (U Relations)/
    18.   Voice of America News and English Broadcasts Wire Service/

Press ? for Help, q to Quit, u to go up a menu          Page: 1/2
```

Note that at the bottom of the screen, it says you're looking at the first of two pages. To move on to the next page, simply press the space bar; to move back type a hyphen ('-').

Finally, pressing RETURN on NASA News will retrieve the file for you and let you read it. You'll have an opportunity to mail the file to yourself (or someone else's email address) or save it into a file.

The Usenet newsgroup `comp.infosystems.gopher` was created for discussions about gopher. The maintainers of the gopher software announce new releases there, and people can ask experienced gopher users for help with problems they've encountered in browsing GopherSpace.

Learning to work your way through GopherSpace is very easy, regardless of which kind of client you happen to be using. You're encouraged to walk around for a bit, to get a feel for what kind of things are hidden inside gopher. Then, when you begin to wonder how in the world you might find something on, say, archaeology, try using veronica.

Veronica

As GopherSpace grew, it became difficult to find things quickly with gopher. The number of new servers grew at a phenomenal rate; consequently, the information you're looking for might be buried fifteen levels down an obscure path.

The staff at the University of Nevada Reno had a brilliant idea—create a tool that will itself help you find things inside of gopher. It took the form of *veronica*,[3] a searchable node in GopherSpace. By selecting '`Other Gopher and Information Servers/`' from the main gopher node, you can opt to search titles in GopherSpace with veronica.

A query of "archaeology" can yield more than fifty hits. While veronica did help you find all of the areas inside of gopher that had to do with archaeology, the search is a raw one—as you make your way down the list, going through what you were able to find, odds are

3. The name "veronica" is a play on the name of "archie," characters in the popular comic strip *Archie*

that a number of the matches will end up being things like Departments of Archaeology at various learning institutions around the world. However, in all likelihood, at least one of the matches will include a wealth of information, including what you originally set out to find.

As a final note, the name "veronica" stands for—take a deep breath—Very Easy Rodent-Oriented Net-wide Index to Computerized Archives. All hail the mighty acronym, it hath struck again.

Netfind: Finding Your Friends

The scope of the Internet often makes it difficult to find the people you want to contact. Michael Schwartz, a professor at the University of Colorado at Boulder, has developed a tool called *netfind* as part of his research on Internet resource discovery.[4] Given the name of the person you're looking for and a rough description of where the person might be (the name of their University or work place, for example), netfind will go out onto the Net and try to find out information about them. It uses a range of methods, from mail-based information to using finger and the domain name system.

A netfind query might look like "`osier zen group`". The first field is the name of the person you're looking for, and subsequent fields are to help netfind make some intelligent guesses about where they might be. The system will next look for domain names that might match `zen` and find the domain `zen.org`.

4. The work that Professor Schwartz has been doing—including measuring the average reachability of hosts on the Internet—makes for fascinating reading. His papers are available on `ftp.cs.colorado.edu` in the directory '`/pub/cs/techreports/schwartz`'.

By using standard mail protocol commands and finger, netfind will likely help you find the address for Jeffrey Osier of The Zen Internet Group. Unfortunately, searches don't always succeed. You may find some domains that have too many hosts for an accurate guess about which system or systems would have the address you're trying to find. In those cases, you can only make a wild guess, but this does sometimes work.

There are a number of netfind servers around the world; if you telnet to `bruno.cs.colorado.edu` or `ds.internic.net` and log in with the account name 'netfind', you'll be given a list of other netfind servers that can be used. It's suggested that you *not* use the one at Colorado, since it tends to be heavily loaded. There is also an extensive offering of online help (along with a more detailed explanation of how netfind works) available from the main netfind menu.

The WHOIS Database

The main WHOIS database is run by the Registration Services part of the InterNIC (see page 129). The `whois` command will let you search a database of every registered domain (e.g., `maine.edu`) and, in some cases, even registered users. It's primarily used by postmasters and system administrators for finding the *Points of Contact* for a site, to let them know of a problem or contact them for one reason or another. You can also find out their postal address. However, many users take advantage of 'whois' to find the domain that may be part of a friend's email address. If we were trying to reach the University of Maine's main network contact, for example, we might use:

```
% whois maine.edu
University of Maine System (MAINE-DOM) Orono, ME 04469

Domain Name: MAINE.EDU       ➥ Domain name

Administrative Contact
  Dube, Gerald F.  (GD72)   DUBE@MAINE.MAINE.EDU
  (207) 581-3505
Technical Contact, Zone Contact:
  Anderson, Irelann Kerry  (IKA)   kerry@maine.maine.edu
  (207) 581-3508


Record last updated on 30-Sep-93. ➥ Last change made to the record

Domain servers in listed order: ➥ Systems that can tell you the
                                     Internet addresses for a site
NAMED.CAPS.MAINE.EDU        130.111.32.11
NAMEP.CAPS.MAINE.EDU        130.111.130.7
NIC.NEAR.NET                192.52.71.4

The InterNIC Registration Services Host contains ONLY Internet
Information
(Networks, ASN's, Domains, and POC's).
.Please use the whois server at nic.ddn.mil for MILNET Information.
```

This information (sought, possibly, by a system administrator) can be used to find out how to contact the University of Maine about a security issue or a problem with connectivity. It's also useful as a way to verify that your guess of the name of a domain is correct before trying to send mail to that site.

As noted at the bottom of the answer we received, the old WHOIS server nic.ddn.mil provides information only about people and organizations in the United States Department of Defense (on the MILNET). If the whois command on your system still sends queries to nic.ddn.mil and not to the new WHOIS server `whois.internic.net`, your support staff or system provider should be contacted about using an updated `whois` program.

Other Uses of WHOIS

Many educational sites run WHOIS servers of their own to offer information about people who may be currently on the staff or attending the institution. To specify a WHOIS server, many implementations include some sort of option or qualifier—in VMS under MultiNet, it's /HOST, in Unix the `-h` command-line switch. To receive information about using the Stanford server from a Unix system, one might use the command `whois -h stanford.edu help`.

A large list of systems offering WHOIS services is being maintained by Matt Power of MIT (`mhpower@athena.mit.edu`). It is available via anonymous FTP from `sipb.mit.edu`, in the directory 'pub/whois'. The file is named '`whois-servers.list`'.

Included on the list are Syracuse University (`syr.edu`), New York University (`acfcluster.nyu.edu`), the University of California at San Diego (`ucsd.edu`), and Stanford University (`stanford.edu`).

"Fingers were made before forks."
— Jonathan Swift, *Polite Conversation*

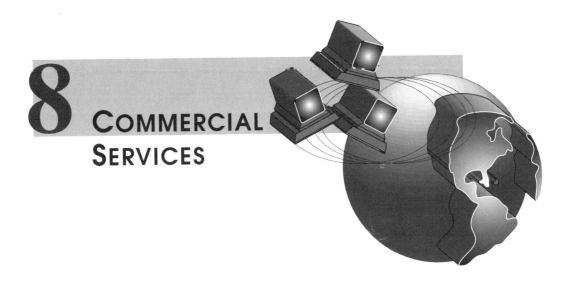

8 COMMERCIAL SERVICES

Many services can be accessed through the Internet. As time progresses and more outlets for commercial activity appear, once-restricted traffic (by the NSFnet Acceptable Use Policy) may now flow freely. Now that there are other networks for that information to travel on, businesses are making their move.

ClariNet e.News

ClariNet is a for-profit electronic publishing network service that provides professional news and information, including live UPI wire service news.

ClariNet lets you read an "electronic newspaper" right on the local system; you can get timely industry news, technology-related wire stories, syndicated columns and features, financial information, stock quotes, and more.

The main distribution mechanism for ClariNet is through a collection of Usenet newsgroups whose names begin with "`clari`". Your system, if it is a subscriber, can receive a feed either directly from ClariNet or from any other news server whose organization is also a subscriber to the service. A subscription is also available via the World Wide Web.

The main feature is *e.News*, an electronic newspaper, gathered live from the wire services of The Associated Press and Reuters. Articles are distributed in 100 newsgroups based on their subject matter and are keyworded for additional topics and the geographical location of the story. *e.News* includes headlines, industry news, box scores, network TV schedules, and more. The main products of *e.News* include:

- *Global and National News,* the general news "paper" with business, national and international news, and sports.

- *TechWire,* special groups for stories on science, technology, and industry stories around them.

- *ClariNet Stock Report,* the stock reports for companies in the areas of computers, telecommunications, and technology.

- *Matrix News,* the electronic newsletter about the world's networks.

- *Newsbytes,* a daily computer-industry news magazine.

- *Syndicated Columns,* including Bizarro (humor) and Views of the World (editorial cartoons).

For full information on ClariNet, including subscription information, contact:

ClariNet Communications Corp.
4880 Stevens Creek Blvd, Suite 206
San Jose, CA 95129-1034 USA
`sales@clari.net`
`http://www.clarinet.com/`
(800) USE-NETS in the United States
(408) 296-0366 elsewhere
(408) 296-1668 Fax

Bunyip Information Services

Bunyip Information Systems Incorporated was formed in January 1992 to create and market a range of network-based tools and information services. The company is a world leader in the research and deployment of innovative technology for the developing Internet marketplace, marketing the successful Archie information distribution system product (already licensed to over 30 sites around the world) as well as contributing numerous technical advances in this fast-changing and highly specialized field. (See page 35 for instructions on how to access their Archie servers.)

Their first product, the well-known Archie system, provides a practical method for distributing information to the fast-growing commercial Internet market. Archie was first deployed in 1991 and has been continually enhanced throughout the past two years. Further information distribution services based upon this software have been developed.

Using their technology and working with representatives from the publishing industry, they created an information distribution mechanism capable of providing authenticated, controlled access to high-quality information across the Internet. Services based upon this technology will distribute collections of books, articles, and other commercial-quality information, all supplemented with a range of computer-enhanced, value-added services, using a simple subscription-based revenue model.

The founders of Bunyip Information Systems developed the Archie information distribution system, the first Internet-based information indexing and distribution service. The Archie software is now licensed by over 30 commercial and academic sites around the world and has proven to be a tremendous success on the Internet. The system has demonstrated the power of information systems in an Internet environment and the value of commercial versions of those programs. Bunyip also provides technical consulting and develops tutorials and documentation.

You can reach the folks at Bunyip by writing or calling:

 Bunyip Information Services
310 Ste. Catherine Street West, Suite 300
Montreal, Quebec
CANADA H2X 2A1
info@bunyip.com
http://www.bunyip.com/
(514) 875-8611
(514) 875-8134 (Fax)

Commercial Databases

 The American Institute of Physics maintains the Physics Information Network. It contains the bibliographic SPIN and General Physics Advanced Abstracts databases. Also available is access to bulletin boards and several

searchable lists (job notices, announcements, etc.). Telnet to `pinet.aip.org`; new users should log in as 'new', with a password of 'new' to register.

Internet Shopping Network

Doing business on the Internet is growing by leaps and bounds. One prime example of this is the *Internet Shopping Network (ISN)*. A division of television's Home Shopping Network, ISN joins hundreds of other companies in offering products for order over the Internet. Using the security features of the Netscape WWW browser, the online shopping service allows people to purchase software, flowers, and even food from the comfort of their own home.

To become a member, simply point your Web browser at the URL `http://www.internet.net/`.[1] You can either provide credit card information by phone or by using the secure Web browser. Using a menu interface, customers can find the products they're interested in, take advantage of current sales, and inquire about special promotions. Minutes later, the order is processed and the product will ship the next business day.

To find out more information, contact ISN at:

Internet Shopping Network
P.O. Box 2187
Menlo Park, CA 94027 USA
`info@internet.net`
`http://www.internet.net/`
(800) 677-7467 in the US
(415) 842-7400 elsewhere

---

1. See "Using the Web" on page 78 for an explanation of how to browse a particular Web page.

B.C.

INTERNET

WILEY'S DICTIONARY

©1995 CREATORS SYNDICATE, INC.   8·10

Online Services

Traditional commercial online services, like CompuServe, have recognized that many of their users also have access to the Internet from home, work, or school and would find it useful to be able to access their accounts through the Internet. In answer to this, it's now possible to access CompuServe, BIX, and GEnie by using `telnet`.

To connect to BIX, simply type `telnet bix.com` and log in as you normally would. Note that a small surcharge will be applied to your BIX account for logging in through the Internet.

For CompuServe, connect to `compuserve.com` and type the name 'cis' as the service and 'LOGON' as the action:

```
% telnet compuserve.com
Trying 198.4.8.2 ...
Connected to compuserve.com.
Escape character is '^]'.

BSDI BSD/386 1.1 (dub-gw-2.compuserve.com) (ttyp7)
```

by johnny hart

THE POTBELLY STOVE OF THE NINETIES.

WILEY'S DICTIONARY

By permission of Johnny Hart and Creators Syndicate, Inc.

```
Host Name: cis

This gateway allows members to access the
CompuServe Information Service directly from the
Internet.  … etc …

Enter choice (LOGON, HELP, OFF): LOGON
```

You will then be asked at what speed you want to receive information and have considered the connect rate for your session. Your account will then be billed the amount for a normal dial-up at that speed. For example:

```
Enter choice (300, 2400, 9600, 14400, OFF): 14400
```

This will bring you to the customary CompuServe 'User ID:' prompt; beginning here, you are connected to CompuServe and should proceed as you would dialing directly with a modem.

Finally, to connect to GEnie, telnet to `hermes.merit.edu` and, at the 'Which Host?' prompt, type

```
Which Host?sprintnet-313171
```

When you are prompted with "U#=", type your GEnie account ID. There will be a surcharge to your GEnie account for using this method; call their customer service department to find out the details.

America Online

For those who don't like to keep their phones tied up while they're logged into America Online, there is another possible solution. If you are able to connect your home computer to the Internet directly (e.g., using a SLIP or PPP dialup connection), you'll also be able to log into AOL without tying up another phone line.

The alternate approach takes advantage of having your personal computer set up to talk with the Internet. Rather than use a modem to dial up, you can instead direct your AOL software to use your existing network connection. By configuring it to use the TCP/IP "modem," your computer will connect directly to AOL over the Internet. Among other things, you'll notice a dramatic reduction in the amount of time needed to log in, and find that transfers also happen at a much faster speed.

If you're interested in taking advantage of this functionality, simply call their customer service department for specific information.

"Needless to say, Aristotle did not envisage modern finance."

— Frederick Copleston, S.J.
A History of Philosophy, v.1

9 THINGS YOU'LL HEAR ABOUT

There are certain things that you'll hear about shortly after you start actively using the Internet. Most people assume that everyone's familiar with them and that they require no additional explanation. If only this were true!

This section addresses a few topics that are commonly encountered and asked about as a new user explores Cyberspace. Some of them are directly related to how the networks are run today; other points are simply interesting to read about.

The Internet Worm

On November 2, 1988, Robert T. Morris, then a graduate student in computer science at Cornell, wrote a self-replicating, self-propagating program called a *worm* and injected it into the Internet. Morris soon discovered that the program was replicating and reinfecting machines at a much faster rate than he had anticipated—there was a bug. Experts also believe that Morris didn't fully understand the reasoning behind what he was attempting. Ultimately, many machines at locations around the country either crashed or became "catatonic." When Morris realized what was happening, he contacted a friend at Harvard to discuss a solution. Eventually, they sent an anonymous message from Harvard over the network, instructing programmers on how to prevent reinfection. However, because the network route was clogged, this message did not get through until it was too late. Computers were affected at many sites, including universities, military sites, and medical research facilities. The estimated cost of dealing with the worm at each installation ranged from $200 to more than $53,000.

The worm took advantage of three weaknesses then present in Unix systems. First, many sites left a debugging option enabled in the network mail agent, *sendmail*, that allowed an outside user to issue privileged commands. Also, a problem with the finger daemon, *fingerd*, which serves `finger` requests (see page 92), allowed the worm to introduce commands to be executed by giving *fingerd* too much information. Finally, the ever-present problem of users choosing poor passwords was vital to the worm's existence— given a limited dictionary of words and common names (like those of possible girlfriends), it could find an impressive number of passwords.

People at the University of California at Berkeley, MIT, and Purdue, to name just a few, had copies of the program and were actively *disassembling* it (turning the program back into its source form) to try to figure out how it worked. Teams of programmers worked nonstop to come up with at least a temporary fix to prevent the continued spread of the worm. After about twelve hours, the team at Berkeley came up with steps that would help retard the spread of the program. Another method was also discovered at Purdue and widely published. The information didn't get out as quickly as it could have, however, because so many sites had completely disconnected themselves from the network.

After a few days things slowly began to return to normal, and everyone wanted to know *who* had done it all. Morris later admitted to John Markoff of *The New York Times* that he was the author, after Markoff received an anonymous tip. Investigation later found sufficient evidence to indict him. In the interim, he was expelled from Cornell.

Robert T. Morris was convicted of a felony under the Computer Fraud and Abuse Act (Title 18 of the United States Code, section 1030). He was sentenced, in May 1990, to three years of probation, 400 hours of community service, a fine of $10,050, and the costs of his supervision—his sentencing was outside of Federal guidelines that suggested a mandatory period of incarceration. His conviction was upheld by the Circuit Court of Appeals, and the Supreme Court declined to hear the case. He is currently working as a programmer (on non-security-related projects) for a Boston-area software company.

A Coke Machine on the Internet?

 Since time immemorial (well, maybe 1970), the Carnegie-Mellon Computer Science Department has maintained a departmental Coke machine, which sells bottles of Coke for a dime or so less than other vending machines around campus. As no Real Programmer can function without caffeine, the machine is

very popular. (It reportedly had the highest sales volume of any Coke machine in the Pittsburgh area.) The machine is loaded on a rather erratic schedule by grad student volunteers.

In the mid-'70s, expansion of the department caused people's offices to be located ever farther away from the main terminal room where the Coke machine stood. It got rather annoying to traipse down to the third floor only to find the machine empty; or worse, to shell out hard-earned cash to receive a recently loaded, still-warm Coke. One day a couple of people got together to devise a solution.

They installed microswitches in the Coke machine to sense how many bottles were present in each of its six columns of bottles. The switches were hooked up to CMUA, the PDP-10 that was then the main departmental computer. A server program was written to keep tabs on the Coke machine's state, including how long each bottle had been in the machine. When you ran the companion status inquiry program, you'd get a display that might look like:

```
EMPTY  EMPTY 1h 3m
COLD   COLD  1h 4m
```

This lets you know that cold Coke could be had by pressing the lower-left or lower-center button, while the bottom bottles in the two right-hand columns had been loaded an hour or so beforehand, so were still warm. (The display changed to just "COLD" after the bottle had been there several hours. The server actually kept track of each bottle's state, though it would only tell you about the bottommost bottle in each column.)

The final piece of the puzzle was needed to let people check Coke status when they were logged in on machines other than CMUA. CMUA's finger server was modified to run the Coke status program whenever someone fingered the nonexistent user 'coke' (see page 92 for more on `finger`). Since `finger` requests are part of standard Internet protocols, people could check the Coke machine from any CMU computer with the command `finger coke@cmua`. In fact, you could discover the Coke machine's status from any machine anywhere on the Internet! Not that it would do you much good if you were a few thousand miles away.

Nothing similar has been done elsewhere, so CMU can legitimately boast of having the only Coke machine on the Internet. (MIT can claim priority on having a computerized Coke machine, but theirs wasn't hooked up to Internet protocols.)

The Coke machine programs were used for over a decade, and were even rewritten for Unix Vaxen when CMUA was retired in the early '80s. The end came in the late '80s, when the local Coke bottler discontinued the returnable, Coke-bottle-shaped bottles. The old machine couldn't handle the nonreturnable, totally uninspired-shape bottles, so it was replaced by a new vending machine. This was right after the New Coke fiasco; the combination of these events left CMU Coke lovers sufficiently disgruntled that no one has bothered to wire up the new machine.[1]

If you're interested in this and other examples of random items attached to the Net, you can use the World Wide Web to discover just how much is being offered. Connect to the URL

---

1. Thanks to Tom Lane (`tom_lane@g.gp.cs.cmu.edu`) for this fantastic anecdote.

```
http://www.yahoo.com/Computers/Internet/
```

and choose "`Interesting Devices Connected to the Net`." You will find refrigerators, coffee machines, hot tubs, and pets. Yes, pets.

The Cuckoo's Egg

First in an article entitled "Stalking the Wily Hacker" and later in the book *The Cuckoo's Egg*, Clifford Stoll described his experiences trying to track down an intruder on a system at the Lawrence Berkeley Laboratory, located in Berkeley, California.[2]

A 75-cent discrepancy in the Lab's accounting records led Stoll on a chase through California, Virginia, and Europe to end up in a small apartment in Hanover, Germany. Stoll dealt with many levels of bureaucracy and red tape and worked with the FBI, the CIA, and the German Bundespost trying to track his hacker down.

The experiences of Stoll, and particularly his message in speaking engagements, all pointed out the dire need for communication among parties on a network of networks. The only way everyone can peacefully coexist in Cyberspace is by ensuring rapid recognition of any existing problems.

Organizations

The indomitable need for humans to congregate and share their common interests is ever-present in the computing world. *User groups* exist around the world, where people share ideas and experiences. Similarly, there are organizations that are one step "above" user groups; that

---

2. See the bibliography for full citations.

is, they exist to encourage or promote an idea or set of ideas rather than to support a specific computer or application of computers.

The Electronic Frontier Foundation

The Electronic Frontier Foundation (EFF) was established to help civilize the "electronic frontier"—the Cyberspace medium becoming ever-present in today's society; to make it truly useful and beneficial not just to a technical elite, but to everyone; and to do this in a way that is in keeping with the society's highest traditions of the free and open flow of information and communication.

The mission of the EFF is

- to engage in and support educational activities that increase popular understanding of the opportunities and challenges posed by developments in computing and telecommunications;

- to develop among policy makers a better understanding of the issues underlying free and open telecommunications, and to support the creation of legal and structural approaches that will ease the assimilation of these new technologies by society;

- to raise public awareness about civil liberties issues arising from the rapid advancement in the area of new computer-based communications media and, where necessary, support litigation in the public interest to preserve, protect, and extend First Amendment rights within the realm of computing and telecommunications technology;

- to encourage and support the development of new tools that will endow nontechnical users with full and easy access to computer-based telecommunications.

There are two Usenet newsgroups, `comp.org.eff.talk` and `comp.org.eff.news`, dedicated to discussion concerning the EFF. They also have mailing list counterparts for those that don't have access to Usenet; to subscribe, write to the addresses `eff-talk-request@eff.org` and `eff-news-request@eff.org`. The first is an informal arena (aka a normal newsgroup) where anyone may voice his or her opinions. The second, `comp.org.eff.news`, is a moderated area for regular postings from the EFF in the form of *EFFector Online*. To submit a posting for the *EFFector Online*, or to get general information about the EFF, write to `eff@eff.org`. There is also a wealth of information available via anonymous FTP on `ftp.eff.org`.

The EFF can be contacted at

The Electronic Frontier Foundation, Inc.
P.O. Box 170190
San Francisco, CA 94117
`ask@eff.org`
`http://www.eff.org/`
(415) 668-7171
(415) 668-7007 (Fax)

The Internet Society

In January 1992, the Internet Society was formed to promote the use of the Internet for research and scholarly communication and collaboration. As a nonprofit organization, the Society hopes to:

■ facilitate and support the technical evolution of the Internet as a research and education infrastructure and to stimulate the involvement of the scientific community, industry, and the public at large;

■ to educate the scientific community, industry, and the public at large concerning the technology, use, and application of the Internet;

■ to promote educational applications of the Internet technology for the benefit of government, colleges and universities, industry, and the public at large;

■ to provide a forum for exploration of new Internet applications, and to stimulate collaboration among organizations in their operational use of the global Internet.

Membership is inexpensive and open to anyone; organizations are strongly urged to join. All organizational members receive discounts for selected Society functions and services, complimentary copies of Society publications, and an opportunity to designate a representative to the Internet Society Advisory Council. More information and applications are available from

The Internet Society
12020 Sunrise Valley Drive, Suite 210
Reston, VA 22091 USA
isoc@isoc.org
http://www.isoc.org/
(800) 468-9507
(703) 648-9888

The Society for Electronic Access

While the Internet is gaining more acceptance among people who are not "techno-wizards" or have to use it as part of their daily work, the amount of information involved in using the Net can have a chilling effect upon its success. While more exposure in the general media does help, crossing class boundaries and making "Cyberspace a better place to live, work, and visit" is not yet a fully realized goal.

The Society for Electronic Access was formed in 1992 by Simona Nass (with some friends) to work towards accomplishing that goal. Its membership is an excellent cross section of society, from the interested public to lawyers, journalists to librarians. They work to make information about legislative computer and telecommunications policy more readily available, and they educate the general public about the Net in general (e.g., how to access and use electronic mail). In addition, media coverage of the Net is tracked by the Society, to aid journalists in researching and developing articles in related areas.

In the past, legislators have declined the opportunity to have constituents reach them through email, for the most part because they don't understand exactly what is involved. The SEA is a valuable resource for these lawmakers; the accurate and useful information the Society provides can help lead to a more informed decision. As the Internet grows in popularity and accessibility, legislators will find that Cyberspace is an even more powerful medium than the conventional telephone or postal service.

Membership in the SEA is open to anyone interested in helping SEA achieve its goals. The primary means of discussion among SEA members is via electronic mailing lists, but you don't have to have email access to become a member. There are a number of working groups in the Society addressing issues ranging from the legal aspects of Cyberspace to how the media is presenting the Net to the world.

To contact the Society for Electronic Access, write to

The Society for Electronic Access
P.O. Box 7081
New York, NY 10116-7081 USA
sea-info@sea.org
http://www.panix.com/sea/
(212) 592-3801

The InterNIC

In January 1993, the NSFnet made a significant step forward in the evolution of the Internet as a coherent body. In the past, the NSFnet Network Service Center (NNSC) was the single point of contact for people seeking information about the Internet, from the very basic to the highly technical. To replace it, the NSFnet created a new group, collectively known as the "InterNIC." At first, three separate companies were awarded contracts to offer three distinct areas of support for the Internet. The new InterNIC began operation on April 1, 1993.

The Registration Services area of the InterNIC, provided by Network Solutions, is responsible for keeping track of Internet numbers so they aren't repeated, register new domain names, and keep track of contacts for those domains. They also maintain the WHOIS database (see page 107 for details on using whois).

The Directory and Database Services area, provided by AT&T, maintains the *Directory of Directories* (see Chapter 9, *Finding Out More*). They maintain a number of databases and operate a gopher server. To find out more, write admin@ds.internic.net.

One particularly useful aspect of the InterNIC's offerings is *The Scout Report*, a weekly publication informing people of new and newly discovered Internet resources. To subscribe to the list, write to the address `majordomo@dsmail.internic.net` with

```
subscribe scout-report
```

in the body of the message. You will receive periodic messages from Susan Calcari, the InterNIC Info Scout, about newly announced tools and services available on the Internet. If you'd rather read the report on the World Wide Web, the URL is

```
http://rs.internic.net/scout_report-index.html
```

The White House

In 1993, the White House Communications Office announced that for the first time in history, the leaders of a major world power would be reachable through Cyberspace. The President and Vice President of the United States have electronic mail addresses:

```
president@whitehouse.gov
vice.president@whitehouse.gov
```

Direct replies from them aren't possible yet—the sheer volume of mail that goes to those two addresses is more than a single person could possibly hope to wade through. Instead, your message will be sorted, and a reply will come through the conventional postal service.

In addition, press releases and other documents are regularly posted to the Usenet newsgroups `alt.politics.usa.misc`, `alt.news-media`, and `talk.politics.misc`, among others. The White House also has a strong presence on a variety of commercial online services, including CompuServe, America Online, and MCI Mail.

If you'd like to receive White House press releases via email, write to the address Publications@Research.ai.mit.edu. In the 'Subject:' header, just include the word "help". The White House Electronic Publication Service will return instructions describing how to receive all of the press releases or only those concerning certain topics (e.g., the economy, foreign policy, etc.). Also, all of this information is available via anonymous FTP from a number of sites, including sunsite.unc.edu in the directory

```
pub/academic/political-science/whitehouse-papers
```

The White House sports a very stylish series of Web pages. To find a wealth of information related to government activity, and learn about the White House and the First Family, point your Web browser at the URL http://www.whitehouse.gov.

GriefNet

Sponsored by Rivendell Resources of Ann Arbor, Michigan, GriefNet is a coordinated series of Web pages, gopher servers, and mailing lists to help people deal with the intensity of grief and major loss. When confronted with the fragility of life, many people go through a wide range of feelings, from confusion to depression to hysteria. Along the same lines, watching a friend or family member go through this prompts you to try to find something you can do to help.

The work of GriefNet was started by Cendra Lynn, Ph.D., a professional psychologist who focuses on the areas of grief and loss. The resources provided by Grief-Net include contact information related to suicide, resources for widows and widowers, concerns about dealing with chronic illness, the reality faced by bereaved parents, and many other topics.

The mailing list `griefnet announce` is maintained to keep people up-to-date about the various activities of GriefNet. To subscribe, write to the address `majordomo@falcon.ic.net` with the line

```
subscribe griefnet-announce your@add.ress
```

in the body of the message, replacing "`your@add.ress`" with your real email address.

For the full collection, point your Web browser at the URL

```
http://www.rivendell.org/
```

or direct your gopher client to the system `rivendell.org`. Both offer a wealth of information. If you have any questions, you can reach Cendra and GriefNet at `griefnet@rivendell.org`.

Text Projects

The wealth of information available to modern researchers is frequently overwhelming—months can be spent in a library trying to track down a few disparate facts. The advent of computers has spurred the development of projects to make books and other information available electronically, thus dramatically reducing the time needed to search for information.

The Online Book Initiative

The Online Book Initiative (OBI) was created to form a publicly accessible repository for the vast collections of books, conference proceedings, reference materials, etc., which can be freely shared.

Beyond machine-readable material, there are huge collections of printed material that could be redistributed if put online. OBI needs people willing to organize informal projects to scan, type, or otherwise get the material into electronic form for inclusion in the Online Book Repository. Library and information scientists are sought to help create formats and structures for organizing the repository.

For further information about the OBI, contact

 Online Book Initiative
Software Tool & Die
1330 Beacon Street
Brookline, MA 02146
obi@world.std.com
(617) 739-0202
(617) 739-0914 (Fax)

Two mailing lists, one for general discussion about OBI issues and another for announcements only, are maintained on world.std.com; write to obi-request@world.std.com to join either list or both.

Project Gutenberg

The purpose of Project Gutenberg is to encourage the creation and distribution of English-language electronic texts. Project Gutenberg assists in the selection of hardware and software as well as in their installation and use. Also, the project helps with scanning, spelling checkers, proofreading, etc. Their goals are to provide a collection of 10,000 of the most used books by the year 2001 and to reduce the effective costs to the user to a price of approximately one cent per book, plus the cost of media and shipping and handling. Thus, the entire cost of libraries of this nature will be approximately $100 plus incidental costs.

In the past, most of the electronic text work has been carried out by private, semiprivate, or incorporated individuals, with several library or college collections being created but being made up mostly of the works entered by individuals on their own time and expense. This labor has largely been either a labor of love or a labor by those who see future libraries as computer-searchable collections that can be transmitted via disks, phone lines, or other media at a fraction of the cost in money, time, and paper as present-day paper media. These electronic books will not have to be rebound, reprinted, reshelved, etc. They will not have to be reserved and restricted to use by one patron at a time. All materials will be available to all patrons from all locations at all times.

The use of this type of library will benefit librarians even more. The amount of information will be so much greater than that available in present-day libraries that people using the library will find it impossible to go it alone—assistance will be imperative for taking full advantage of what is available.

All interested parties are welcome to get involved with the creation and distribution of electronic texts, whether it's a commitment to typing, scanning, proofreading, collecting, or whatever your pleasure might be.

The system `mrcnext.cso.uiuc.edu` is home to the archives of Project Gutenberg; under the directory '`/pub/etext`' you'll find masterpieces like *Peter Pan*, *Alice in Wonderland*, and *Paradise Lost*. Each piece added to the Gutenberg collection undergoes a thorough and complete copyright check to ensure that it's legally redistributable. They also maintain a Web page at

```
http://jg.cso.uiuc.edu/PG/welcome.html
```

For more information on Project Gutenberg, write to

Project Gutenberg
Illinois Benedictine College
5700 College Road
Lisle, IL 60532-0900
hart@vmdcso.uiuc.edu
http://jg.cso.uiuc.edu/PG/welcome.html

Project Runeberg

In Sweden, a similar project was formed to carry free electronic editions of classic Nordic literature and art. Just as Project Gutenberg carries free electronic English texts, so Project Runeberg is the equivalent for Scandinavian languages. The name of Project Runeberg was chosen, in part, because it contains a number of the works by Johan Ludvig Runeberg; his work *Fänrik Ståls sägner* was the first text added to the collection. Soon after, other works in Finnish and Swedish were added. The word "Runeberg" can be interpreted as a mountain ("berg") of runes (letters of the old Scandinavian alphabet). Finally, "Runeberg" was chosen because it is easily represented on computers—using accented or umlauted characters on computers can often cause problems for users.

First typed in by hand, the texts in Project Runeberg later began to be formed by use of Optical Character Recognition (OCR) software. This made it possible to put printed text on a computer in considerably less time, albeit with some difficulty. OCR software can sometimes misread a word, thus requiring a person to proofread what the computer thinks it saw. However, the time required to perform this copyediting is small compared to manually typing in the body of the text.

The collections for Project Runeberg are available via anonymous FTP from ftp.lysator.liu.se in the directory '/pub/runeberg', and on the World Wide Web at the URL http://www.lysator.liu.se/runeberg/

If you have any questions or would like to help with the project, you can write to

Project Runeberg
Lysator
Linköpig University
S-581 83 Linköpig
Sweden
`runeberg@lysator.liu.se`
+46 13 126498 by phone

Advances in Networking

Research and development are two buzzwords often heard when discussing the networking field—everything needs to go faster, over longer distances, for a lower cost. To "keep current," one should read the various trade magazines and newspapers or frequent the networking-oriented newsgroups of Usenet. If possible, attend trade shows and symposia like Usenix, Interop, etc.

*Global
SchoolNet*

The Global SchoolNet Foundation, a nonprofit organization, is a major contributor to the philosophy, design, culture, and content of educational networking on the Internet.

Among their many projects is the Global SCHLnet Newsgroup Service. Global SCHLnet brings information about the many Global SchoolNet (formerly FrEd-Mail) curriculum projects, resources, and services. SCHLnet takes the form of a series of Usenet newsgroups distributed only to specific sites. The fees for a SCHLnet newsfeed are used to cover the active moderation of those groups.

If your site cannot afford to subscribe to the SCHLnet newsfeed, there is another option. The `schl.call.ideas` newsgroup carries information about various online projects. To receive a free selection of the best projects posted to that group, write to `majordomo@acme.fred.org` with the message "`subscribe ideas-list`" in the body of the message.

Global SchoolNet also manages a number of general mailing lists for K-12 teachers to join on a no-fee basis. The lists include the Global Grocery List project, which collects information from around the world about the prices of items from a list of products. For example, a class will travel to their local grocery stores, recording the prices of items on the grocery list, then share their prices with other participating classes from around the world. The end result of this collection is current data that can be used in math, social studies, science, and health classes. To receive copies of the past lists, use anonymous FTP to `ftp.dpi.state.nc.us` and receive the files in the directory '`/pub/Global.Grocery.List`' directory.

In an effort to promote student and instructor participation in data telecommunications, CERFnet (the California Education and Research Federation Network) developed a prototype gateway between CERFnet and the Global SchoolNet Network. The gateway uses file-serving capabilities based on the Usenet model of conferences and selected news feeds, allowing a great deal of flexibility in linking Global SchoolNet users with other networks and educators on other systems all over the world. Fifteen selected Global SchoolNet sites will dial up directly to their local CERFnet terminal server, which will act as the regional file server. In the prototype phase, out-of-state Global SchoolNet hubs would be linked directly to the server in San Diego via toll-free telephone calls.

*"An earlier version of this novel appeared two years ago
as a manicotti recipe on the Internet."*

CERFnet also wants to promote this prototype gateway to colleges and universities that want to serve their own local K-12 communities. Their vision is one of a national network of university academic computing labs that act as local file servers to their regional K-12 Global SchoolNet sites, using existing facilities and transportation networks.

For more information about the Global SchoolNet Foundation, write to the address `fred@acme.fred.org`.

NREN

In December 1991, Congress passed the High Performance Computing and Communications (HPCC) Program. It will accelerate the development of a thousandfold improvement in useful computing capability and a hundredfold improvement in available computer communications by 1996. It comprises four components: high-performance computing, development of new software technology and algorithms, better education and research support, and a gigabit network.

The fourth component, the National Research and Education Network (NREN), will have approximately 1000 times the present capacity of existing technology. It is for research and education, not general-purpose communication. Nonetheless, it will be fundamentally dependent upon its use as a testbed for new communications technologies. Enhanced image visualization and distributed computing will help with problems like medical diagnosis, aerodynamics, and global change. A collaborative effort between U.S. industry, the federal government, and the educational community should help usher in a new era in computing that will leave its mark on every facet of modern society.

A mailing list, `nren-discuss@psi.com`, is available for discussion of the NREN; write to `nren-discuss-request@psi.com` to be added. For a booklet describing the HPCC, write to

Federal Coordinating Council
   for Science, Engineering and Technology
Committee on Physical, Mathematical, and
   Engineering Sciences
c/o National Science Foundation
Computer and Information Science and
   Engineering Directorate
1800 G Street, N.W.
Washington, DC 20550

Internet Talk Radio

The Internet now has its own global radio station, in the form of the Internet Talk Radio (ITR). Fashioned after similar conventional radio programs, ITR presents interviews and news stories about the Internet exclusively in electronic form.

Created by Carl Malamud, Internet Talk Radio has been mentioned in "normal" press, like *The Wall Street Journal* and *The New York Times*, and even discussed on its counterpart, National Public Radio. ITR is distributed as a set of (rather large) audio files which can be played on a variety of systems, including workstations from Sun Microsystems.

Regular features of ITR include "Geek of the Week," a traditional interview format with industry leaders and well-known net.citizens; the Incidental Tourist,[3] which offers restaurant reviews and travel tips for cities around the world; TechNation, a one-hour weekly radio show focusing on Americans and technology; and some occasional book reviews. New features are being developed for ITR on a regular basis—a close relationship with the National Press Club led to the first-ever Press Club luncheon broadcast on the Internet. For many people, these luncheons are not very visible; they need to be there, own a satellite dish, or subscribe to a cable provider who carries CSPAN. TechNation has featured such distinguished guests as Dr. Linus Pauling, two-time winner of the Nobel Prize, and Jane Metcalfe and Louis Rossetto, the editors and publishers of *Wired* magazine.

The ITR is based on the Internet multicast backbone (the *MBONE*). If you want to learn more about the

---

3. The Incidental Tourist is a play on the title of Anne Tyler's fantastic book *The Accidental Tourist*, which I urge everyone to read.

MBONE, you can retrieve a frequently asked questions list about it from `venera.isi.edu` in the directory '`/mbone`' as '`faq.txt`'.

Each set of files in an ITR distribution is taped in the same professional environment that you would expect from typical radio—high-quality microphones, digital recorders, and top-of-the-line sound mixers. The files themselves are distributed around the Internet on a number of FTP sites. Write to `info@radio.com` for the latest information. To find out how to play the files on your system, ask your system administrator or support staff for assistance.

Online Career Center

The Online Career Center database offers access to job listings and full-text resume files with online keyword searches to assist both employers and individuals in effectively using the Internet. Forty leading corporations in the United States have joined to create a non-profit organization to develop and manage the Career Center.

There are no charges for people to access the more than 8,000 job listings, view company information and profiles, enter resumes into the company-sponsored database, or email resumes to potential employers. You may also receive career assistance information on subjects like career fairs, job searches, resume writing, and other career resources.

To access the database, use gopher to connect to `occ.com`. (See page 101 to learn how.) For more information on the Online Career Center, contact

William O. Warren
Executive Director
Online Career Center
3125 Dandy Trail
Indianapolis, IN 46214
occ-info@occ.com
http://www.occ.com/occ/
(317) 293-6499

"To talk in publick, to think in solitude, to read and to hear, to inquire, and to answer inquiries, is the business of a scholar."

— Samuel Johnson,
Chapter VIII
The History of Rasselas, Prince of Abissinia

10 FINDING OUT MORE

Furthering your network education will be a challenge without some tips on where to look. In the realm of freely redistributable information, there are three main sources of information: the InterNIC Directory of Directories, a continuing attempt to catalogue the many resources available on the Net; MaasInfo, a well-composed set of files providing facts (and some strong opinions) about what's out there; and Requests for Comments, the Internet standards.

In the area of published work (aside from what you're holding), *The Matrix* by John Quarterman is invaluable if you want to know how the different networks are connected and who's responsible for what. An updated edition of O'Reilly and Associate's *Directory of Electronic Mail Addressing and Networks* offers information similar to that offered in *The Matrix* but doesn't go into as much depth on how the networks fit together. Rather, it gives you information on how to contact the administrators of each network. To learn about computer networking in general, Andrew Tanenbaum's *Computer Networks* is an excellent text. Finally, to teach how the Internet protocols themselves operate, Douglas Comer wrote a series of books entitled *Internetworking With TCP/IP,* which discuss every aspect of the TCP/IP protocol suite.

Keep your eyes open—in the coming years, the information gap will be closing drastically. The technology is here, and people are willing to learn. The body of documentation will continue to grow by leaps and bounds.

Magazines and Newsletters

[With the growing interest about the Internet in the publishing industry, a number of magazines are now entirely devoted to covering the Net or have regular columns about it. In addition, according to Neal Stephenson in *The New Republic*, in June, July, and the first half of August of 1993, "major American newspapers carried 173 stories mentioning the Internet, compared with twenty-two a year earlier." This, combined with coverage in such truly mainstream publications as *Spin Magazine, The Atlantic,* and *Newsweek,* is a strong indicator that the Net has begun to breech the barrier separating usage of the Internet from the public at large. Indeed, the press coverage of the Net has grown to astronomic proportions. In 1994 at year's end, the total number of articles in magazines and newspapers reached well over 75,000. A few of the available magazines and newsletters are mentioned here—keep an eye on the newsstands, though, since many more will be appearing in the future.

Internet
World

Internet World, published by the Mecklermedia Corporation, is a rich resource for Net surfers. Issues are monthly and cover a variety of topics, from new developments on the Internet (e.g., new services) to a spotlight on a particular service provider. Edited by Michael Neubarth, each issue of *Internet World* proves to be very well written and interesting. It originally started out as a newsletter with distribution primarily among librarians and researchers; it has since been transformed into a mainstream glossy magazine with a very professional look. For subscription information, contact:

Internet World
P. O. Box 713
Mt. Morris, IL 61054-0713 USA
`iwsubs@kable.com`
`http://www.mecklerweb.com/mags/iw/iwhome.htm`
(800) 573-3062 in the United States
(815) 734-1261 elsewhere

NetGuide

Published by CMP Media, *NetGuide* joined the ranks of magazines that cover the Internet and the growing prominence of Cyberspace in the world culture. They sport a remarkable collection of information, ranging from games played on the Net to solving problems users most commonly encounter when they're online to the legal issues that are raised as the Internet goes through its fundamental growing pains during adolescence. Throughout the magazine, you'll find references to gopher and FTP sites, Usenet newsgroups, and World Wide Web pages—with URLs listed even in their advertisements. As Cyberspace expands even further and the Internet increases in its possibilities, the presence of mainstream magazines continues to convince people that this new form of communication is here to stay. *NetGuide* should be available at a local bookstore; to subscribe to the magazine, contact them at:

NetGuide
600 Community Drive
Manhasset, NY 11030 USA
`netmail@netguide.cmp.com`
`http://techweb.cmp.com/net/`
(800) 829-0421 in the United States
(904) 445-4662 ext. 420 elsewhere

InfoBahn

While most magazines present the technical and fundamental aspects of the Net, *InfoBahn* was started to pay full attention to the cultural and intellectual issues. An underlying aspect of the Net as a whole is the impact it is having on daily life. In *InfoBahn*, readers are able to find out about what's lying beneath the enthusiasm and publicity they encounter every day. The magazine addresses the current issues, like the growing commercialization of the Internet, the added presence of the world's governments in attempted regulation and control, and the effects of the availability of explicit sexual material. Rather than pay attention to the top-level points of interest, *InfoBahn* puts its readers in touch with the long-term effects of this new culture we've created.

InfoBahn is still in its infancy, yet appears to be a much-needed addition to the magazines that cover the developing counterculture. To subscribe, write to:

InfoBahn
Postmodern Communications, Inc.
985 East Hillsdale Blvd., Suite 88
Foster City, CA 94404-2112 USA
`subscribe@postmodern.com`
`http://www.postmodern.com/`
(415) 438-2191
(415) 286-9518 (Fax)

Matrix News

Matrix Information and Directory Services, Inc., publishes a monthly newsletter called *Matrix News*. It discusses "the Matrix," the term for all of the computer networks worldwide that exchange electronic mail. Coverage includes Usenet, FidoNet, BITNET, the Internet, and conferencing systems like the Well and CompuServe. The newsletter is edited by John S. Quarterman (author of the very successful book *The Matrix*) and Smoot Carl-Mitchell.

What sets *Matrix News* apart from many other periodicals is its distribution method—you can either get copies in paper form or you can receive it electronically. The publishers ask people not to redistribute copies they receive electronically, since it is not free and doing so would only make it more difficult to continue publishing the newsletter. They also publish through ClariNet (which was discussed in Chapter 8 *Commercial Services*), through the Usenet newsgroup `clari.matrix_news`.

You can also receive the *Matrix Maps Quarterly*; in addition to a regular subscription to *Matrix News*, you will receive full-color maps of the Internet's connectivity, size, growth, and other information.

To subscribe, write to

Matrix Information and Directory Services, Inc.
1106 Clayton Lane, Suite 500W
Austin, TX 78723
`mids@tic.com`
`http://www.tic.com/mids/mn.html`
(512) 451-7602
(512) 452-0127 (Fax)

Planète
Internet

The Internet consists not of a particular circle of sup-
porters, but of a wide and diverse collection of interested
parties around the world. The international nature of
the Net is underscored by the continued attention of the
global media. One prime example of this is *Planète
Internet*, a mainstream magazine in France. Produced
as the first French magazine about the Internet, their
work concentrates on four major areas.

The magazine works to explain the general issues
related to the Net: what it is, how it works, where it
came from, and what can be found with a little effort.
The articles present readers with a fundamental understanding of this new technology.

Coupled with the general description is a collection
of stories regarding the human aspects of online communication. Rather than look at specific instances, *Planète
Internet* tries to discover how the Net impacts everyday
life. In part, the work addresses the question of who is
shaping whom: Is the Net being crafted by the people
using it, or are their habits and cultures being directly
impacted by its use?

In response to the growing commercialization of the
Net, the magazine includes descriptions of how companies can benefit from the Internet, how to address security issues, and what tools are available to corporations
to make the Internet an integral part of their business
plan.

Finally, French resources on the Internet are
detailed for the French audience. Readers who are
familiar with the French language will find this an
intriguing collection, proving once again how the Net
has taken down the walls that separate the many cultures of the world.

If you'd like to subscribe to *Planète Internet*, the publisher, Net Press, can be reached at:

Net Press
16-24 rue Louis Pasteur
92100 Boulogne - France
`editor@netpress.fr`
`http://www.netpress.fr/`
+33 1 46 05 77 17
+33 1 46 04 22 20 (Fax)

Internet Columns

As the Internet makes its way into the corners of computing, more industry periodicals are recognizing that their readers are discovering the Net and need to know more about it. Among them are two magazines that previously catered mainly to people running private bulletin board systems (BBSes) and commercial online services.

The first, *Boardwatch Magazine*, includes articles about the Internet, ranging from news and legal items that affect the Internet community to informational articles about how to use FTP, gopher, and other tools. Edited by Jack Rickard, *Boardwatch* is a must for any Net surfer's library.

Contact them at:

Boardwatch Magazine
8500 West Bowles Ave., Suite 210
Littleton, CO 80123
`subscriptions@boardwatch.com`
`http://www.boardwatch.com/`
(800) 933-6038 in the United States
(303) 973-6038 everywhere
(303) 973-3731 (Fax)

The second magazine of interest, *Online Access*, carries a column by Michael Strangelove covering many aspects of the Net. The bulk of its content is geared towards customers of major online services like CompuServe and Prodigy. Nonetheless, their regular Internet column and frequent features on special topics (e.g., the NREN and efforts to connect grade schools to the Net) are well worth the cost of an issue.

You can write to them for more information at

 Online Access Magazine
920 N. Franklin, Suite 203
Chicago, IL 60610-9588
`Online_Access@portal.com`

Note that both *Boardwatch* and *Online Access* are probably available on your local newsstand or in a local bookstore, if you'd like to look at an issue before arranging for a subscription.

News Articles

 The continuing coverage of the Internet in the print media has an interesting effect: there's too much for one person to read. In answer to this challenge, Educom, a consortium of colleges and universities, created *Edupage*, a condensed collection of news articles about information technology.

Three times a week, you will receive a summary of the news articles thus far. Five or six top stories, coupled with a few related stories, are summarized to give you a snapshot of the current developments. The list is a must for anyone wishing to stay in touch with the growth and expansion of Cyberspace.

Each noted article mentions the source newspaper or magazine and the publication date. You can then use this information to either get a full copy of the source magazine or paper through conventional means or include it in citations of stories related to a particular research topic.

To subscribe, write to `listproc@educom.edu`; in the body of the message, put the line "`subscribe edupage` *Your Name*" in the body of the message, replacing *Your Name* with your full name, not your email address. To cancel your subscription, send mail to the same address containing the text "`unsubscribe edupage`".

InterNIC Directory of Directories

Until 1993, the NSF Network Service Center (NNSC) compiled the Internet Resource Guide (IRG). The goal of the guide was to increase the visibility of various Internet resources that may help users do their work better. While not an exhaustive list, the guide proved to be a useful compendium of many resources and a helpful reference for a new user.

In 1993, the Directory and Database Services area of the InterNIC merged the IRG into its own *InterNIC Directory of Directories*. The original information included in the IRG, ranging from library catalogs, network contact information, and supercomputer availability, is all included in the new Directory. A new format, coupled with the latest information and new subject areas, makes the InterNIC directory a highly useful body of work. To find out about updates to the list, write `admin@ds.internic.net`.

The *Directory of Directories* is available via anonymous FTP from `ds.internic.net` in the directory '`/dirofdirs`'. It is split into various subdirectories based on subject area (e.g., '`archive`', '`ftpsite`', etc.). The original IRG is available in the directory '`/resource-guide`'.

To access the directory on the World Wide Web, point your browser at the URL

```
http://www.internic.net/ds/dsdirofdirs.html.
```

Electronic Journals

 The Association of Research Libraries (ARL) publishes a hard-copy directory of electronic journals, newsletters, and scholarly discussion lists. Written by Ann Okerson, the directory is a compilation of entries for hundreds of scholarly lists, dozens of journals and newsletters, and many other titles, including newsletter-digests, into one reference source. Each entry includes instructions for accessing the referenced publication or list.

The directory, along with a compilation by Diane Kovacs called *Directories of Scholarly Electronic Conferences*, is available either electronically (via gopher and the URL listed below) or in print from:

 Office of Scientific & Academic Publishing
Association of Research Libraries
21 Dupont Circle NW
Suite 800
Washington, DC 20036
`osap@cni.org`
`gopher://arl.cni.org/11/scomm/edir`
(202) 296-2296
(202) 872-0884 (Fax)

The ARL is a nonprofit organization representing over 100 research libraries in the United States and Canada.

The MaasInfo Package

Robert E. Maas wrote a set of documents, collectively known as *MaasInfo*, that provides a good overview of how to use some of the services available over the Internet. He describes how to telnet directly to an NNTP port on a system if Usenet isn't available locally, how to use Archie, and gives quick instructions on how to get started with listservs, how to use FTP, and other topics.

He also details information related to using networks. The most intriguing portion of his package is the "TopIndex"—a compilation of most of the known indexes to electronic information. It mentions things like the nixpub Public Access Unix list, technological societies and organizations, plus dozens of other topics. An excellent collection of network-oriented bibliographies is also included.

The package used to be available via anonymous FTP. The most up-to-date version is now available on the World Wide Web at the URL

```
http://pip.shsu.edu/ftp/MaasInfo/MaasInfo.TopIndex.html
```

John December's Internet CMC List

John December of the Rensselaer Polytechnic Institute maintains a list of information services concerning Internet and computer-mediated communication (CMC). This useful guide is a gold mine; it includes pointers to files, services, and books about the Internet and CMC-related topics. Sections include The Internet and Services, Information Services and Electronic Publications, Societies and Organizations, and a Selected Bibliography. I urge everyone to regularly read this document.

The list is available via anonymous FTP either in plain text or in Postscript. FTP to `ftp.rpi.edu` and look in the '`/pub/communications`' directory; the file '`internet-cmc.readme`' describes the format of each of the files that are available. You can also find the list on the Web at

```
http://www.rpi.edu/Internet/Guides/decemj/icmc/top.html
```

The Web page has three separate choices for browsing the list; of the possibilities, '2-level' is recommended as an entry point to its use.

Send any comments or questions about CMC or the Web page to John December at `decemj@rpi.edu`.

Requests for Comments

The internal workings of the Internet are defined by a set of documents called RFCs (Request for Comments). The general process for creating an RFC is for someone wanting something formalized to write a document describing the issue and mail it to Jon Postel (`postel@isi.edu`). He acts as a referee for the proposal. It is then commented on by all those wishing to take part in the discussion (electronically, of course). It may go through multiple revisions. Should it be generally accepted as a good idea, it will be assigned a number and filed with the RFCs.

There is a subset of RFCs called the FYIs (For Your Information documents). They are written in a language much more informal than that used in the other, standard RFCs. Topics range from answers to common questions for new and experienced users to a suggested bibliography.

Finally, as the Internet has grown and technology has changed, some RFCs have become unnecessary. These obsolete RFCs cannot be ignored, however. Frequently, when a change is made to some RFC that causes a new one to obsolete others, the new RFC contains only explanations and motivations for the change. Understanding the model on which the whole facility is based may involve reading the original and subsequent RFCs on the topic.

RFCs and FYIs are available via FTP from many sources, including:

- The `ftp.internic.net` archive, as '`/rfc/rfcxxxx.txt`', where *xxxx* is the number of the RFC.

- from `ftp.uu.net`, in the directory '`/inet/rfc`'.

They're also available via electronic mail by sending mail to the address `mailserv@rs.internic.net` with a '`Subject:`' line of document-by-name `rfcxxxx` (again, *xxxx* is an RFC number). To learn about archive servers, consult Appendix C, *Retrieving Files via Email.*

"Knowledge is of two kinds. We know a subject ourselves, or we know where we can find information upon it."

— Samuel Johnson
Letter to Lord Chesterfield
February, 1755

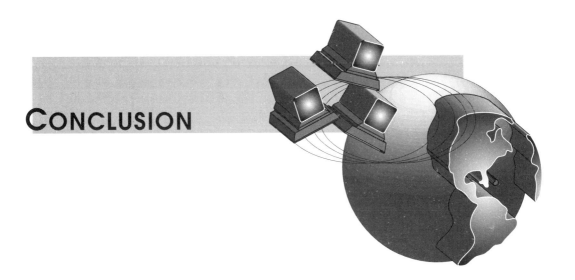

CONCLUSION

The Internet changes daily (if not hourly); this guide is simply a snapshot in time, certainly omitting some aspects of the Net. However, you should now have enough information to make the incredible breadth and complexity of the Internet a mite less imposing. Coupled with some exploration and experimentation, every user has the potential to be a competent net.citizen, using the facilities that are available to their fullest.

You, the reader, are *strongly* encouraged to suggest improvements to any part of this guide. If something was unclear, left you with doubts, or wasn't addressed, it should be fixed. Please report any problems or inaccuracies to guide-bugs@zen.org. A Web page is being maintained with all corrections for the book between printings; direct your Web browser at the URL http://www.zen.org/fourth/.

If you are interested in discussion about information to be included or removed from this guide, write to `guide-request@zen.org` to be placed on a mailing list for such things.

"I've seed de first an de last. . . ; I seed de beginnin, en now I sees de endin. . ."
— William Faulkner
The Sound & The Fury
April 8, 1928

A THE KIDS ON THE NET

Cyberspace is becoming a noticeable part of many households. Children are finding themselves in the intriguing position of teaching their parents how to use their own computer: how to send email, connect to fun Internet sites, and how to use the World Wide Web.

Similarly, parents find a unique joy in sitting down with their children and showing them this amazing new world, where they can talk with people far, far away and get information at the click of a button. Teachers are incorporating the "Information Superhighway" into their classrooms; lessons have expanded to include live-action examples of a particular topic. During recess a child will be laughing with another about something they found on the Net the evening before.

Indeed, many parents are very comfortable letting their children go surfing around the Net, feeling confident that they'll discover a never-ending supply of fruitful information that will contribute to their learning process.

As time progresses, the reality of what Cyberspace holds comes into play. News stories about children being lured over the Net by complete strangers to meet them or take a trip on the promise of great fun chill these parents to the bone. They realize that as with any part of society, there are those who cast a dark shadow on an otherwise peaceful setting. Even in the cases where this new electronic "friendship" is free from danger, kids should be taught that strangers are just that: strangers. The age-old advice of not accepting candy from someone on the street rings true online as well.

The online world sports the ability to send graphic images back and forth, sharing drawings and photographs, among other things. A great controversy hit the Net in early 1995 when it was discovered that child pornography was also being distributed electronically. Not only is such material objectionable ethically, but in most countries citizens are explicitly forbidden to possess or distribute material that exploits children. The danger of encountering a pedophile online is just as present as in everyday life—more so, in fact. Given the limitations of online communications, it's often difficult to sense that someone should be avoided.

This confronts parents with the questions, "How can I let my children use the Net in a safe setting? Should I let them use it at all?" The answer to the first question is much easier to answer than the second. Many people, including me, would encourage parents to consider introducing their children to the Net but do it with some caution. Given the impact the online world is having on daily life in many areas, kids in grade school today will be entering the workforce facing the expectation that they already have fundamental experience in electronic communications of one sort or another. I believe that helping children acquaint themselves with the rising technology at this point in their lives will have substantial dividends farther down the road.

A Safe Online Presence

The first and foremost rule to teach your child when letting him or her use any online service is this: Do not give out any personal information. No phone numbers, no addresses, no specific details that could let someone figure out where the child goes to school, shops, or plays. Public message areas are the chief examples of places to withhold this type of information. Only send email with those details when you are certain that you know and have complete trust in the person receiving it. If your child is using a "chat" area on an online service, always avoid giving out your last name if you can. It's often best to sit with your child, monitoring the discussions as they occur.

If your child makes a new friend over the Net, then tries to arrange to meet in person, always make sure that you go along. The meeting should be in a very publicly visible area, and during daylight times. While it's possible to meet the type of person that you expect, Cyberspace has the interesting side effect of allowing people to hide behind their screen, presenting themselves as an entirely different person. For example, someone may claim to be a child and in reality be a middle-aged adult, or a man may tell you he is a woman. Really feel that you know the person before you allow your child to meet them.

The National Center for Missing and Exploited children has an excellent pamphlet entitled *Child Safety on*

FoxTrot

the Information Highway. It includes a sheet that you can tear out and paste up on your monitor, with "My Rules for Online Safety." It provides six basic rules for your child to agree to follow before actively using the Internet or any online service. You can receive a free copy by writing or calling

> National Center for Missing and Exploited
>   Children
> 2101 Wilson Boulevard, Suite 550
> Arlington, VA 22201-3052 USA
> `http://www.scubed.com:8001/`
>   `public_service/ncmec.html`
> (800) 843-5678 in the United States
> (703) 235-3900 otherwise

Web Pages for Children

There are dozens of Web pages that were specifically designed to be of interest to children. There are also others that have information for parents, ranging from advice on different aspects of raising a child to contact

by Bill Amend

information for adoption agencies, missing children hotlines, etc. Keep looking—as time passes, the explosive growth of the Web will include new and innovative offerings for children.

➧ http://www.xmission.com/~wwwads/sharware.html

To have your kids age 3 or older play with your computer and really learn how to use it, check out *Bert's Coloring Programs*. It offers shareware programs for drawing pictures of things, including African animals, Christmas, dinosaurs, prehistoric animals, and whales and dolphins. You can also get Rachel's Fashion Dolls, a children's paper doll dress-up and coloring program.

➧ http://www.bev.net/education/SeaWorld/homepage.html

If travel is not always possible, a "virtual" visit to SeaWorld would certainly be nice.

➧ http://www.hcc.hawaii.edu/dinos/dinos.1.html

The Honolulu Community College offers the first unique, free, permanent exhibit of dinosaur fossils available over the Internet.

`http://gagme.wwa.com/~boba/kids.html`

For a ton of fun, look at *Uncle Bob's Kid's Page*. It's a remarkably complete catalogue of online information that kids will find interesting and entertaining.

 `http://www.pd.astro.it/local-cgi-bin/kids.cgi/forms`

Presented from Italy, *The Children's Page* was written and designed specifically for kids to enjoy. It's regularly updated with new Web discoveries, like learning about frogs or solving the mystery of volcanoes.

 `http://www.ucalgary.ca/~dkbrown/`

The Children's Literature Web Guide in Canada has features ranging from the home pages of authors of children's books to selections of children's writings, as well as a vast collection of recommended reading.

 `http://www.cochran.com/tt.html`

The Canadian TV series *Theodore Tugboat* is about a cheerful tugboat who likes to be friends with everyone. Life in his playful Big Harbour community is always changing, and whatever each new day brings, Theodore likes to do the things that friendly tugboats do. There's lots to see and do with Theodore and his many floating friends.

 `http://scitech.lm.com/`

Doctor Duey's Wacky Web Pages let kids go walking on a nature trail, choosing the directions that they want to take in their exploration.

 `http://robot0.ge.uiuc.edu/~carlosp/color/`

In *Carlos' Coloring Book* you just pick a picture, pick a color, and then click where you want that color to be used. In an instant, your mouse becomes a virtual crayon and part of your picture is filled in!

On `http://www.zen.org/~brendan/kids.html` you will find a current list of information for and related to children. They range from fun sites to facts for parents (e.g., dealing with child abuse or facts on adoption) to educational Web pages.

Classroom Connect

Wentworth Worldwide Media publishes a near-monthly newsletter, *Classroom Connect*. It is a teacher's gold mine. Each issue provides sample lesson plans that involve using the Internet as part of the classroom, including Web pages to visit and gopher sites that have information related to various topics. Teachers are able to have messages included as part of the '`keypals@`' connection, where schools seek pen pals for a particular class. Similarly, the Classroom Connect Meeting Place allows people to try to share projects or get help from others in their area of interest. For example, a teacher teaching about the Middle Ages might seek to have the class engage in a live chat with someone who happens to own a real castle.

There is a Classroom Connect mailing list that makes it possible for schools to talk to each other in a common setting with similar goals, similar to the published Meeting Place. To join the list, write to the address `info@wentworth.com` with

`subscribe CRC your@add.ress` in the body of the message.

To subscribe to the *Classroom Connect* newsletter, contact:

Wentworth Worldwide Media, Inc.
1866 Colonial Village Lane
P.O. Box 10488
Lancaster, PA 17605-9981 USA
connect@wentworth.com
http://www.wentworth.com/
(800) 638-1639 in the United States
(717) 393-1000 otherwise
(717) 393-5752 Fax

B GETTING TO OTHER NETWORKS

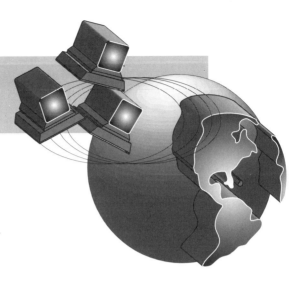

Interconnectivity has been and always will be one of the biggest goals in computer networking. The ultimate desire is to make it so one person can contact anyone else no matter where they are. A number of gateways between networks have been set up. They include the following.

America Online	To reach a user on AOL, address your mail as *userid*`@aol.com`; make sure you take out any spaces in the AOL "screen name" when figuring out the *userid*.
AppleLink	General Electric sells access to AppleLink, an online service oriented to Apple computer users. It has the email address: *user*`@applelink.apple.com`.

ATTMail	AT&T sells a commercial email service called ATT-Mail. Its users can be reached by writing to `user@attmail.com`.
BIX	Users on BIX (the Byte Information eXchange) can be reached at `user@bix.com`.
CompuServe (CI$)	To reach a user on the commercial service CompuServe, address the mail with `xxxxx.xxx@compuserve.com`, where *xxxxx.xxx* is the user's CompuServe user ID. Normally CompuServe IDs are represented as being separated by a comma (like 71999,141); since most mailers don't react well to having commas in addresses, it was changed to a period. For the above address, mail would be sent to `71999.141@compuserve.com`.
EcoNet	EcoNet is a community of persons using networks for information sharing and collaboration with respect to environmentally oriented

programs. Members of Eco-Net can be reached with the address *user*`@igc.apc.org`.

FidoNet	The FidoNet computer network can be reached by using a special addressing method. If John Smith is on the node '`1:2/3.4`' on FidoNet, his email address would be `john_smith@p`**`4`**`.f`**`3`**`.n`**`2`**`.z`**`1`**`.fido net.org` (notice how each of the numbers falls in place?).
GEnie	General Electric Information Services runs GEnie, a commercial service offering many round-table discussions on a variety of topics, online air reservations, and other services. Contact users on GEnie by writing to *user*`@genie.geis.com`.
GeoNet	Customers of the GeoNet mail service can be reached at the system they are on. For users in North America, write to *user*`@geo4.geonet.de`; in the United Kingdom, use *user*`@geo2.geonet.de`; and Europe, write to *user*`@geo1.geonet.de`.

MCI Mail	MCI also sells email accounts (similar to ATT-Mail). Users can be reached by referring to their user ID number; it's guaranteed to be unique. Addresses take the form `1234567@mcimail.com`.
PeaceNet	Users on the PeaceNet network can be reached by writing to `user@igc.apc.org`.
Prodigy	The Prodigy online service boasts the most subscribers of any commercial service in the United States. Write to Prodigy users by addressing mail to `userid@prodigy.com`.
The Well	Users on the online service The Well can be reached by writing to `user@well.sf.ca.us`. The Well is directly connected to the Internet.

WWIVnet	WWIVnet is a network of personal computers all running the WWIV BBS software. On WWIVnet, users are referred to as `user@node`. To reach them from the Internet, use
	`node@station.mv.com.`

Note that some services are not (nor do they plan to be) accessible from the "outside" (like Prodigy); others, like GEnie and America Online, are actively investigating the possibility of creating a gateway into their system. America Online is developing a package that will allow users to connect over the Internet on their PC. Ask your local support staff about any possibility of using such a package locally.

For the latest information on mailing to various networks, consult a list called the *Inter-Network Mail Guide*. It's available from `ftp.csd.uwm.edu` in the file '`/pub/internetwork-mail-guide`'. To find out if you can directly connect to a given commercial service through the Internet, your best chance for accurate information is to ask the service itself, through its customer service line.

C RETRIEVING FILES VIA EMAIL

For those who have a connection to the Internet but cannot use FTP, there do exist a few alternatives to get those files you so desperately need. When requesting files, it's imperative that you keep in mind the size of your request—odds are the other people who may be using your link won't be too receptive to sudden bursts of really heavy traffic on their normally sedate connection.

Archive Servers

An alternative to the currently much-overused FTP-mail system is taking advantage of the many *archive servers* that are presently being maintained. These are programs that receive email messages which contain commands and act on them. For example, sending an archive server the command `help` will usually yield, in the form of a piece of email, information on how to use the various commands that the server has available.

One such archive server is `mailserv@internic.net`. Maintained by the Resource Services part of the InterNIC, the server is set up to make all of the information at the NIC available for people who don't have access to FTP. This also includes the WHOIS service (see page 107). Some sample '`Subject:`' lines for queries to the InterNIC server are:

```
Subject: help
  Describes available commands.

Subject: document-by-name rfc822
  Sends a copy of RFC-822.

Subject: document-by-name rfc-index
  Sends an index of the available RFCs.

Subject: netinfo domain-template.txt
  Sends a domain application.

Subject: whois maine
  Sends WHOIS information on 'maine'.
```

More information on using their archive server can be obtained by writing to `mailserv@internic.net` with a '`Subject:`' of '`help`'.

There are different "brands" of archive server, each with its own set of commands and services. Among them there often exists a common set of commands and services (e.g., `index`, `help`, etc.). Be that as it may, one should always consult the individual `help` for a specific server before assuming the syntax—100-kilobyte surprises can be hard on a system.

FTP-by-Mail Servers

Some systems offer people the ability to receive files through a mock FTP interface via email. See Chapter 3, *Anonymous FTP*, for a general overview of how to use FTP. The effects of providing such a service vary, although a rule of thumb is that it will probably use a substantial amount of the available resources on a system.

The "original" FTP-by-Mail service, BITFTP, is available to BITNET users from the Princeton node PUCC. It was once accessible to anyone, but had to be closed to non-BITNET users because of the heavy load on the system.

In part because of this closure, Paul Vixie announced the existence of a package called FTPmail. Originally available only on a system at the Digital Equipment Corporation, FTPmail is now maintained on number of sites. They include:

`ftpmail@census.gov`	(USA)
`ftpmail@ftp-gw-1.pa.dec.com`	(USA)
`ftpmail@sunsite.unc.edu`	(USA)
`ftpmail@cs.uow.edu.au`	(Australia)
`ftpmail@grasp.insa-lyon.fr`	(France)
`ftpmail@ftp.uni-stuttgart.de`	(Germany)
`ftpmail@ieunet.ie`	(Ireland)
`ftpmail@ftp.luth.se`	(Sweden)
`ftpmail@doc.ic.ac.uk`	(United Kingdom)

Write to any of the servers with 'help' in the body of the letter for instructions on its use. You will be able to control different aspects of the server's response, ranging from its format, the size of each message, and the address to which the reply should be sent. The first answer you'll receive will tell you exactly what commands will be executed and how many requests are ahead of yours in the queue. Be aware that there can often be hundreds, if not thousands, of other messages being processed by the FTP-mail server.

If you'd rather try another server, check the response you received; it's likely to include instructions on how to use the FTPmail `delete` command to cancel your request. You can then submit the query to another server.

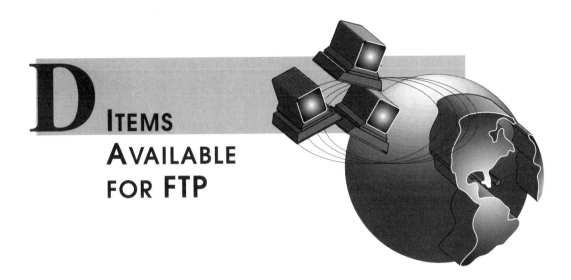

D ITEMS AVAILABLE FOR FTP

What follows is a listing of the "FTPable items" that are mentioned in this book; they are listed in the order of their appearance. For more information on actually retrieving them, read Chapter 3, *Anonymous FTP*.

Interest Groups

ftp.internic.net */netinfo*	The file `interest-groups` is a full listing of nearly every known mailing list.

Listserv

cs-ftp.bu.edu */pub/listserv*	An implementation of the list-serv system for Unix is available; it emulates much of the functionality of its BITNET counterpart.

FAQs

| rtfm.mit.edu /pub/usenet | The RTFM archives include the Frequently Asked Questions lists for nearly every Usenet newsgroup. The filenames are simply their 'Subject:' headers with underscores in place of spaces. There are also truncated filenames, in case your system can't handle really long names. |

St. George

| ftp.cerf.net /internet/resources/ library_catalog | The file internet-catalogs has a date suffix indicating the most recent version of the St. George Directory. It also includes information on Internet BBSes and other things. |

Internet Services List

| ftp.csd.uwm.edu /pub | Scott Yanoff's list of Internet services is stored in the file 'inet.services.txt'; it's also posted regularly to the Usenet newsgroups alt.bbs.internet and alt.internet.services. |

HYTELNET

ftp.usask.ca **/pub/hytelnet**	Versions of the HYTELNET program are available for IBM PCs, Unix-based systems, and Vaxen running VMS. To use the program on your PC, you must have the appropriate software and hardware needed to do a telnet.

NIST Guide

csrc.ncsl.nist.gov **/pub/nistir**	A guide to using the NIST computer security BBS is available as the file `bbsguide.txt`.

WAIS Software

ftp.wais.com **/pub**	Software and documentation for the Wide Area Information Servers.

WHOIS List

rtfm.mit.edu **/pub/whois**	Matt Power's list of sites offering WHOIS services is stored in the file `whois-servers.list`.

ClariNet e.News

ftp.clarinet.com **/info**	This directory houses information on the ClariNct *e.News* service.

EFF

ftp.eff.org **/pub/EFF**	Information on the Electronic Frontier Foundation, including back issues of *EFFector Online* and *EFFnews*, is available, along with the EFF mission statement and related documents.

Project Gutenberg

mrcnext.cso.uiuc.edu **/etext**	Project Gutenberg offers the free texts of books like *Peter Pan* and *Alice in Wonderland*.

MBONE

venera.isi.edu **/mbone**	The frequently asked questions list for the Internet multicast backbone (the "MBONE") is available in the file 'faq.txt'.

Directory of Directories

ds.internic.net **/dirofdirs**	The InterNIC *Directory of Directories* is divided into various subject areas. It includes the information that was contained in the now-defunct Internet Resource Guide.

RFCs

ftp.internic.net **/rfc**	The Internet Requests for Comments are available on the NIC; some of them, including the FYI series, will be of interest to new users. The files 'fyi-index.txt' and 'rfc-index.txt' list the topics of each FYI/RFC, and 'std-index.txt' lists the title of each RFC that is also an Internet standard.

Internet CMC

ftp.rpi.edu */pub/communications*	John December's fantastic list of information sources about the Internet and computer-mediated communication.

Internet Mailing Guide

ra.msstate.edu **/pub/docs**	The Guide provides the nitty-gritty for going "from here to there"—it is updated semiregularly.

Jargon File

prep.ai.mit.edu **/pub/gnu**	The Jargon File, an online compendium of network lore, is in the file 'jargon*nnn*.ascii.z', where *nnn* is the latest version. *The New Hacker's Dictionary* is based upon this file.

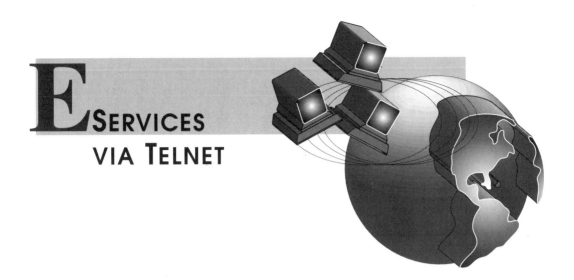

E SERVICES VIA TELNET

When the second edition of *Zen* came out, one of the most common requests I had was to include an appendix, similar to the previous one, listing all of the "telnetable services" named in the book. I encourage you to get a copy of Scott Yanoff's list of Internet services (see page 62 for the details) for the latest information on what you can access over the Net.

AIP

| **pinet.aip.org**
new | Log in as `new` with a password of `new` to use the Physics Information Network at the American Institute of Physics. You will need to register. |

APA

| **eis.calstate.edu**
bbs | A BBS run by the American Philosophical Association. |

Air Pollution

| **ttnbbs.rtpnc.epa.gov**
none | A BBS run by the United States Environmental Protection Agency. Press the Return key once to start your session. |

Archie

| **archie.sura.net**
archie | Log in as `archie` to use the Archie database. |

BIX

| **bix.com** | The BIX commercial online service. |

Clemson Forestry and Agriculture

| **eureka.clemson.edu**
PUBLIC | Information about forestry and agriculture, mainly of the Southeastern United States. |

CompuServe

| **compuserve.com**
cis | The CompuServe commercial online service. |

Dante Project

library.dartmouth.edu **connect dante**	The Dartmouth College Dante Project.

Denver University

nyx.cs.du.edu **new**	The NYX BBS in Colorado.

E-Math

e-math.ams.com **e-math**	The American Mathematical Society (AMS).

FDA

fdabbs.fda.gov **bbs**	The United States Food and Drug Administration.

FEDIX

fedix.fie.com **fedix**	Information on scholarships, fellowships, minority colleges and universities, etc.

Freenet

freenet-in-a.cwru.edu	You don't need a login ID initially when connecting to the Cleveland Freenet; rather, it will walk you through a registration process.

GEnie

hermes.merit.edu *sprintnet-313171*	The GEnie commercial online service.

Geographic Server

geoserver.eecs. umich.edu *port 3000*	Find out information by city, zip code, etc.

Gopher

consultant.micro. umn.edu *gopher*	An account that will let you try the Internet gopher.

Ham Radio Callbook

callsign.cs.buffalo.edu *port 2000*	Information on ham radio call signs, searchable by different criteria.

Knowbot

nri.reston.va.us *port 185*	Lets you search the White Pages directory.

LawNet

lawnet.law. columbia.edu *lawnet*	Online law library, info on law firms, the U.S. courts, and a gateway into HYTEL-NET.

	NASA Extragalactic Database
ned.ipac.caltech.edu *ned*	The NASA/IPAC database on extragalactic objects.

	NASA SpaceLink
spacelink.msfc. nasa.gov *guest*	Space-related information, including NASA news.

	NICOL
nicol.jvnc.net *nicol*	Information on JVNCnet, its members, and other Internet activities. Also access to the Meckler MC(2) electronic information service.

	Net Mail Sites
hermes.merit.edu *netmailsites*	Search for a given university, company, or other network party to find out their email address.

	Netfind
bruno.cs.colorado.edu *netfind*	A netfind server; also try `netfind.oc.com`.

Newton

newton.dep.anl.gov *bbs*	A BBS for people teaching or studying science, math, or computer science. NOT related to the Newton hand-held computer.

OCEANIC

delocn.udel.edu *INFO*	An interactive database of research information covering all aspects of marine studies.

PENpages

psupen.psu.edu *WORLD*	Database of agricultural information.

Rutgers University

quartz.rutgers.edu *bbs*	A popular BBS run by Rutgers.

STIS

stis.nsf.gov *public*	National Science Foundation publications, grant request forms, etc.

University of Iowa

bbs.isca.uiowa.edu *guest*	The ISCA bulletin-board system.

UNC Chapel Hill

launchpad.unc.edu *launch*	A BBS run by the folks at the University of North Carolina.

WAIS

quake.think.com *wais*	An account that will let you do WAIS searches.

Washington University

library.wustl.edu *services*	A gateway into a huge array of online services available over the Internet.

Weather Service

downwind.sprl. umich.edu *port 3000*	A database of weather and related information, including current weather and forecasts; located at the University of Michigan.

Weather Service

wind.atmos.uah.edu *port 3000*	Another weather server, from the University of Alabama at Huntsville.

F

COUNTRY CODES

$\mathbf{T}$his appendix lists the known country codes as defined in the ISO-3166 standard.

af	Afghanistan	ag	Antigua
al	Albania	ar	Argentina
dz	Algeria	am	Armenia
as	American Samoa	aw	Aruba
ad	Andorra	au	Australia
ao	Angola	at	Austria
aq	Antarctica	az	Azerbaijan

bs	Bahamas	**bv**	Bouvet Island
bh	Bahrain	**br**	Brazil
bd	Bangladesh	**io**	British Indian Ocean Territory
bb	Barbados	**bn**	Brunei
by	Belarus	**bg**	Bulgaria
be	Belgium	**bf**	Burkina Faso
bz	Belize	**bi**	Burundi
bj	Benin	**kh**	Cambodia
bm	Bermuda	**cm**	Cameroon
bt	Bhutan	**ca**	Canada
bo	Bolivia	**ct**	Canton and Enderbury Islands
ba	Bosnia-Hercegovina	**cv**	Cape Verde
bw	Botswana	**ky**	Cayman Islands

cf	Central Africia Republic	**cy**	Cyprus
td	Chad	**cz**	Czech Republic
cl	Chile	**dk**	Denmark
cn	China	**dj**	Djibouti
cx	Christmas Island	**dm**	Dominica
cc	Cocos (Keeling) Islands	**do**	Dominican Republic
co	Columbia	**tp**	East Timor
km	Comoros	**ec**	Ecuador
cg	Congo	**eg**	Egypt
ck	Cook Islands	**sv**	El Salvador
cr	Costa Rica	**gq**	Equatorial Guinea
ci	Cote d'Ivoire	**ee**	Estonia
hr	Croatia	**et**	Ethiopia
cu	Cuba	**fk**	Falkland Islands

fo	Faroe Islands	**gl**	Greenland
fj	Fiji	**gd**	Grenada
fi	Finland	**gp**	Guadeloupe
fr	France	**gu**	Guam
gf	French Guiana	**gt**	Guatemala
pf	French Polynesia	**gn**	Guinea
tf	French Southern Territories	**gw**	Guinea-Bisseu
ga	Gabon	**gy**	Guyana
gm	Gambia	**ht**	Haiti
ge	Georgia	**hm**	Heard and McDonald Islands
de	Germany	**hn**	Honduras
gh	Ghana	**hk**	Hong Kong
gi	Gibraltar	**hg**	Hungary
gr	Greece	**is**	Iceland

in	India	**kp**	Demo. People's Rep. of Korea
id	Indonesia	**kr**	Republic of Korea
ir	Iran	**kw**	Kuwait
iq	Iraq	**kg**	Kyrgystan
ie	Ireland	**la**	Lao People's Demo. Republic
il	Israel	**lb**	Lebanon
it	Italy	**ls**	Lesotho
jm	Jamaica	**lr**	Liberia
jp	Japan	**ly**	Libyan Arab Jamahiriya
jo	Jordan	**li**	Liechtenstein
kz	Kazakhstan	**lt**	Lithuania
ke	Kenya	**lu**	Luxembourg
ki	Kiribati	**mo**	Macau

mg	Madagascar	**mn**	Mongolia
mw	Malawi	**ms**	Montserrat
my	Malaysia	**ma**	Morocco
mv	Maldives	**mz**	Mozambique
ml	Mali	**mm**	Myanmar
mt	Malta	**na**	Namibia
mh	Marshall Islands	**nr**	Nauru
mq	Martinique	**np**	Nepal
mr	Mauritania	**nl**	Netherlands
mu	Mauritius	**an**	Netherlands Antilles
mx	Mexico	**nt**	Neutral Zone
fm	Micronesia	**nc**	New Caledonia
md	Moldova	**nz**	New Zealand
mc	Monaco	**ni**	Nicaragua

ne	Niger	**ph**	Philippines
ng	Nigeria	**pn**	Pitcairn Island
nu	Niue	**pl**	Poland
nf	Norfolk Island	**pt**	Portugal
mp	Northern Mariana Islands	**pr**	Puerto Rico
no	Norway	**qa**	Qatar
om	Oman	**re**	Re'union
pk	Pakistan	**ro**	Romania
pw	Palau	**ru**	Russian Federation
pa	Panama	**rw**	Rwanda
pg	Papua New Guinea	**sh**	St. Helena
py	Paraguay	**kn**	St. Kitts Nevis Anguilla
pe	Peru	**lc**	Saint Lucia

pm	St. Pierre and Miquelon	**so**	Somalia
vc	St. Vincent and the Grenadines	**za**	South Africa
ws	Samoa	**es**	Spain
sm	San Marino	**lk**	Sri Lanka
st	Sao Tome and Principe	**sd**	Sudan
sa	Saudi Arabia	**sr**	Suriname
sn	Senegal	**sj**	Svalbard and Jan Mayen Islands
sc	Seychelles	**sz**	Swaziland
sl	Sierra Leone	**se**	Sweden
sg	Singapore	**ch**	Switzerland
sk	Slovakia	**sy**	Syria
si	Slovenia	**tw**	Taiwan
sb	Solomon Islands	**tj**	Tajikistan

tz	Tanzania	**ae**	United Arab Emirates
th	Thailand	**gb**	United Kingdom
tg	Togo	**us**	United States
tk	Tokelau	**pu**	U.S. Misc. Pacific Islands
to	Tonga	**uy**	Uruguay
tt	Trinidad and Tobago	**uz**	Uzbekistan
tn	Tunisia	**vu**	Vanuatu
tr	Turkey	**va**	Vatican City State
tm	Turkmenistan	**ve**	Venezuela
tc	Turks and Caicos Islands	**vn**	Vietnam
tv	Tuvalu	**vg**	Virgin Islands (British)
ug	Uganda	**vi**	Virgin Islands (U.S.)
ua	Ukraine	**wf**	Wallis and Futuma Islands

eh	Western Sahara	**zr**	Zaire
ye	Yemen	**zm**	Zambia
yu	Yugoslavia	**zw**	Zimbabwe

G WRITING A HOME PAGE

After discovering the World Wide Web, many people find themselves compelled to craft their own home page. While the time involved in learning the intricacies of HTML is often quite a deterrent, the basic steps can allow you to present a rather impressive Web page without taking up too much of your free time.

Odds are many of your friends who are on the Net have faced a similar challenge—presenting, with great pride, their own creation to the world. Teamwork can be invaluable when you're exploring the Internet. Learn to ask each other questions whenever you can't quite figure out how to present something in your home page. Much of the Web is comprised of HTML experimentation; there's not necessarily only one way to offer a piece of information. Try new techniques as you get more comfortable writing with your imagination, rather than using a specific approach.

When a Web browser reads a file from a server, its actions are sometimes chosen by the name of the file it's asked to retrieve. The extension at the end of the filename is often '.html', though DOS servers will offer them as '.htm'. This extension directs the browser to interpret the file's contents as being encoded with HTML commands. For example, you can tell the browser to make certain words appear in bold or italic, present a bulleted list, or make a few words be a link to another Web page.

The power behind the World Wide Web lies in this ability to cross-reference information from one site to another. That way, it's easy to group random Web pages in a style that makes the offerings more user-friendly.

Viewing Home Pages

As you're working on your home page, you can see how it looks and test that it's written correctly by directing the browser directly to the file you're editing. With most browsers, the *File* pull-down menu offers an *Open File* option to open a specific filename on your system. By choosing the file you're currently editing, you can revisit the page after you make each adjustment or addition with the *Reload* button.

If you're curious how a certain page was able to display itself in a certain way, most Web browsers include the ability to view the "HTML source" to the visited page. Under the *View* pull-down menu on some browsers, you will find a *Source* option to look at the raw HTML text. Many people use this as an excellent way to learn how to write their own pages—by seeing the detailed approach of others. The text-based browser lynx will show you the source by typing a '\' character.

When you are ready to present your Web page to the world, you will need to put it in an area that your site's Web server knows how to reference. There's usually a directory tree (or folder, on a Macintosh) that houses the publicly accessible Web pages. The name in a URL directs the server to where the file would be located.

Many home pages are cited by a URL that looks like:

```
http://www.zen.org/~sven/
```

The '~sven/' part tells the server to look in the home directory for the user 'sven' on a Unix system for a sub-directory called 'public_html'. Under that will be the file 'index.html', the default file that's attempted when a URL refers to a directory instead of a specific file-name. Ask your system administrator, system pro-vider, or local support staff for instructions on how to make your home page available to everyone through their Web server.

Writing in HTML

Every Web page has a fundamental design to it. All need to have this basic structure:

```
<html>
<head>
<title>The Home Page Title</title>
</head>
<body>

The text to appear on the Web page.

</body>
</html>
```

You may be surprised that the Web page is written in flat text, not created with a fancy word processor.[1] The underlying style of HTML is plain text; it sometimes refers to files that contain images, or uses commands that affect the graphical presentation of the page. Yet the layout of the low-level information conveyed from a Web server to a browser for a Web page is written in this basic format.

A page written in HTML is comprised of two separate sections: the head and the body. The latter is where you'll do most, if not all, of your writing. The actions for a Web page result from *tags* used in the text. Two tags are required: '`<html>`' to start the page and '`</html>`' to end it.

Tags

Each tag is enclosed in '`<`' and '`>`' as '`<command>`', with no spaces between the command and its enclosing less-than and greater-than signs. Most of the commands come in pairs. For instance, the body section is started with '`<body>`' and finished with the command and a leading slash in '`</body>`'. The most common mistake you'll encounter when writing in HTML is forgetting to close a particular section.

In the head section, you'll usually have only the '`<title>`' command, which tells the browser how to name the window the person is looking at. Many graphic programs include a bar along the top giving the name of the application that's running. Web browsers use this to display the name of the Web page that's being visited.

In the body lies the text that's shown inside the browser's window. There are many possible commands you can use within your text to improve how it looks.

---

1. However, some companies are releasing versions of their editors that do include the ability to generate a copy of the file with HTML notation.

It should be noted that the case does not matter for tags. They can be in uppercase, lowercase, or a mix of both. Thus, '`<body>`', '`<BODY>`', and '`<BoDy>`' are all equivalent.

Text Formatting

A useful type of command is one which controls the formatting of a piece of text. To make words appear in italics, you'll use the commands '`<i>`' and '`</i>`'. Thus, a line of HTML written with

```
They played some <i>fantastic</i> music!
```

will appear on the browser as

They played some *fantastic* music!

As you can see, the HTML source of the page looks very flat compared to what the user will see.

Other types of text formatting you can use include:

- `<b>...</b>`
  Make the text be in bold.

- `<u>...</u>`
  Underline the text.

- `<var>...</var>`
  Show a word or words as being a variable.

- `<tt>...</tt>`
  Present the text in a typewriter font.

- `<em>...</em>`
  Show the text for emphasis.

- `<strong>...</string>`
  Provide more emphasis than `<em>`.

The text in the body section is not displayed verbatim. Lines are pressed together, regardless of how they're typed in the HTML file. Thus, even if you have a line separated from another with an empty line, the browser will show them flowing together. The text

```
Some of my favorite movies are:
  <i>Casablanca</i>
  <i>An Affair to Remember</i>
  <i>Sleepless in Seattle</i>
  <i>Dangerous Minds</i>
```

will be shown on the browser as

> Some of my favorite movies are: *Casablanca An Affair to Remember Sleepless in Seattle Dangerous Minds*

To counter this, you can always force a new paragraph with '`<p>`', or force a line break with '`<br>`'. Thus, the text above rewritten as

```
<p>Some of my favorite movies are:
<p><i>Casablanca</i><br>
  <i>An Affair to Remember</i><br>
  <i>Sleepless in Seattle</i><br>
  <i>Dangerous Minds</i><br>
```

makes the text be separated into

> Some of my favorite movies are:
>
> *Casablanca*
> *An Affair to Remember*
> *Sleepless in Seattle*
> *Dangerous Minds*

The '`<p>`' and '`<br>`' tags are two of the few commands that, for historic reasons, don't need to have closing counterparts, though '`</p>`' and '`</br>`' are valid.

You will use the '`<p>`' tag fairly often. By presenting what you write as separate paragraphs, you will make the information more readable. The typical use looks like:

```
<p>The trip to Ireland was fantastic.  When we
arrived at the pub, we discovered that …
<p>Little did we know the musician would play an
extra set!  It wasn't until after three in the
morning …
```

The story that will be presented will have each paragraph separated by some space, to make the paragraphs easily distinct. Again, without '`<p>`' the lines would all run together in one large paragraph.

Headings   You can show section headings with different character sizes. This makes it possible to cle arly display sections and subsections. The tags vary in size from '`<H1>`', the largest, through '`<H6>`' for the smallest. Each is closed out with '`</H1>`' through '`</H6>`'. The most common use of these tags is to present the Web page separated by topic:

```
<h1>Folk Music</h1>
<h3>Stan Rogers</h3>
<h3>John Gorka</h3>
<h1>Rhythm &amp; Blues</h1>
<h3>Brian White</h3>
<h3>Wendy and Lisa</h3>
```

The result would be a page looking like

Folk Music
Stan Rogers
John Gorka
Rhythm & Blues
Brian White
Wendy and Lisa

Each heading has space separating it from text above and below it. You will note the strange '&' part of one of the second main section headings. Since HTML uses certain characters as part of its command text, you will need to use these commands instead:

&	Ampersand '&'
<	Left bracket '<'
>	Right bracket '>'
"	Double quotes

If you want double quotes to appear in the text without having to use this special command, you can use single quotes like:

```
''Do you know where they went?'' she asked.
```

This will appear on the browser as having joined quotes:

"Do you know where they went?" she asked.

Hypertext Links

One of the more common uses of HTML is to refer to another area of the page, some other page on that system, or a different site entirely. The idea behind a "hypertext" language is the ability to make a given item—a word, a picture, and so forth.—point to a separate piece of information.

In HTML, this is accomplished with the *anchor* tag, which takes the form of '`<a href=''URL''>`*text*`</a>`'. The second part with '`href`' is called an *attribute* for the tag, offering a detail that can help the browser decide what to do with the information. There are other attributes available for anchors, but '`href`' is the most common.

In the anchor tag, the *URL* piece contains the pointer to the named Web page. The *text* is the word or words that appear highlighted, inviting the user to select it to follow the link. For instance, the line

```
<a href=''http://www.zen.org/~sven/''>Sven Heinicke</a>
```

makes it possible to visit Sven's home page by clicking on the words Sven Heinicke.

To refer to a file in the same area as the file for your home page, you don't need to type out the entire URL. Instead, just refer to the filename in a *partial* URL:

```
<a href=''music.html''>my favorite music</a>
```

The browser will understand how to retrieve it in the same location as the referring page.

And finally, use 'mailto' inside the 'href' to make it possible for the person visiting the Web page to send mail to a particular address when a given item is selected:

```
<a href=''mailto:brendan@zen.org''>Brendan Kehoe</a>
```

One challenge when adding these anchor tags is to keep them current. It's often the case that another site may change the location of a Web page, a user may no longer have an account there, or the Web server will change machines. This can lead to confusion when a user is consulting your Web page, and they're told the URL they've chosen to follow is invalid. Try to get into the habit of occasionally verifying that the links you refer to are still in working order.

Lists of
Information

HTML also provides the ability to note a series of information in a variety of forms: a bulleted list or a numerical list, among others. This is often useful when you've got a number of categories to mention, or a long list of Web sites that you want to tell people about.

For a bulleted list, the items are surrounded by '`<ul>`' and '`</ul>`' (referring to an "*u*nordered *list*"). Each entry is noted with the '`<li>`' command. Using the movie list we referred to earlier, you can create a bulleted version with:

```
Some of my favorite movies are:
<ul>
   <li><i>Casablanca</i>
   <li><i>An Affair to Remember</i>
   <li><i>Sleepless in Seattle</i>
   <li><i>Dangerous Minds</i>
</ul>
```

The person visiting the Web page will then see:

Some of my favorite movies are:

- *Casablanca*
- *An Affair to Remember*
- *Sleepless in Seattle*
- *Dangerous Minds*

Similarly, if you used '`<ol>`' and '`</ol>`' in that example instead of '`<ul>`' and '`</ul>`', it will create an "*o*rdered *list*:"

Some of my favorite movies are:

1. *Casablanca*
2. *An Affair to Remember*
3. *Sleepless in Seattle*
4. *Dangerous Minds*

There are other possible kinds of lists, including those offering word definitions (definition being set off from the word being defined), and a list resembling a directory on a disk. However, the bulleted and itemized lists are the kinds you'll want to use as a starting point.

Images

A large majority of Web pages available today are composed not only of words, but also of graphic images. The can be stylistic art, like a colored dot instead of a small black one for a list, or a three-dimensional block across the screen separating sections; an image representing another Web page's contents; a picture of the person who wrote the Web page; or art drawn related to the page's topic.

These images are usually stored in GIF or JPEG files named '`file.gif`' and '`file.jpg`', respectively. To include such a file as part of your Web page, use the tag '`<img src=''family.gif''>`'. The '`src`' attribute refers the server to the file you want to have displayed. That will allow graphic browsers to display the picture of your family when they visit your Web site. Don't forget that there are people who have text-only browsers and thus can't see images. To make a text browser not leave a blank space where the image would have appeared, add the '`alt`' attribute, as an alternative to showing the image:

```
<img src=''family.gif''  alt=''[A picture of my family]''>
```

While the second attribute is not absolutely necessary, there are many people who will be happy that you took them into account when you were designing your home page.

Final Notes

As you may have noticed in bookstores, popularity of the Web and HTML are growing by leaps and bounds. There are a number of books dedicated entirely to the intricacies of HTML. Rather than try to reproduce all of that in a single appendix, the author encourages readers to browse their local bookstore and choose one of the many Web books that are now available.

The possibilities of what your home page could offer are limited only by your own imagination. When creating a Web page, remember to present the information in a form that will be understandable by others—using obscure terms, forgetting to include the link to a site you're mentioning, or trying to minimize what you've written will only lead to confusion with the person reading your home page.

But most importantly, have fun writing it. What you've created may be visited by thousands of people around the world, underscoring the universal communication offered by the Internet. Enjoy the inspirations and discovery the Web can bring to you.

GLOSSARY

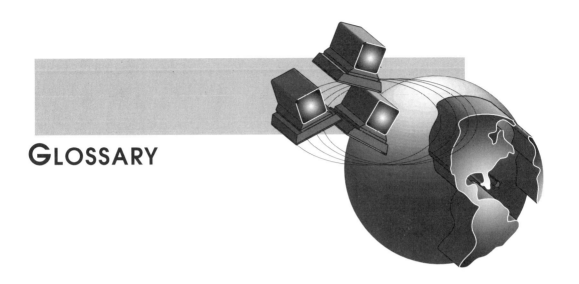

This glossary is only a tiny subset of all of the various terms and other things that people regularly use on the Net. For a more complete (and very entertaining) reference, it's suggested you get a copy of *The New Hacker's Dictionary*, which is based on a very large text file called the Jargon File. Edited by Eric Raymond (`eric@snark.thyrsus.com`), the dictionary is available from the MIT Press, Cambridge, Massachusetts, 02142; its ISBN number is `0-262-68069-6`. For FTP information on the Jargon File, consult Appendix D, *Items Available for FTP*. Also see RFC-1392, the *Internet Users' Glossary*, for a less-entertaining but highly useful glossary.

`:-)` This odd symbol is one of the ways a person can portray mood in the very flat medium of computers—by using "smilies." This is "metacommunication," and there are literally hundreds of smilies, from the obvious to the obscure. This particular example expresses happiness. Don't see it? Tilt your head to the left 90 degrees. Smilies are also used to denote sarcasm. There are actually a few small booklets on smilies available in many bookstores.

address resolution Conversion of an Internet address to the corresponding physical address. On an Ethernet, resolution requires broadcasting on the local area network.

administrivia Administrative tasks, most often related to the maintenance of mailing lists, digests, news gateways, etc.

anonymous FTP Also known as "anon FTP"; a service provided to make files available to the general Internet community—see Chapter 3, *Anonymous FTP*.

ANSI American National Standards Institute. Disseminates basic standards like ASCII and acts as the United States delegate to the ISO. Standards can be ordered from ANSI by writing to the ANSI Sales Department, 1430 Broadway, New York, NY 10018.

aphasia Loss or impairment of the power to use or comprehend words, usually resulting from brain damage.

Archie A service that provides lookups for packages in a database of the offerings of countless of anonymous FTP sites. For a full description of Archie and its offerings, see page 35.

archive server An email-based file transfer facility offered by some systems.

ARPA (Advanced Research Projects Agency) Former name of DARPA (Defense Advanced Research Projects Agency), the government agency that funded ARPAnet and later the DARPA Internet.

ARPAnet A pioneering long-haul network funded by ARPA. It served as the basis for early networking research as well as a central backbone during the development of the Internet. The ARPAnet consisted of individual packet-switching computers interconnected by leased lines. The ARPAnet no longer exists as a singular entity.

asynchronous Transmission by individual bytes, not related to specific timing on the transmitting end.

auto-magic Something which happens pseudoautomatically and is usually too complex to go into any further than to say it happens "automagically."

backbone A high-speed connection within a network that connects shorter, usually slower, circuits. Also used in reference to a system that acts as a hub for activity (although those are becoming much less prevalent now than they were ten years ago).

bandwidth The capacity of a medium to transmit a signal. More informally, the mythical "size" of the Net and its ability to carry the files and messages of those that use it. Some view certain kinds of traffic (FTPing hundreds of graphics images, for example) as a "waste of bandwidth" and look down on them.

BITNET (Because It's Time Network)   An international educational network that is now slowly disappearing.

bounce   The return of a piece of mail because of an error in its delivery.

btw   An abbreviation for "by the way."

browser   A software package used to access the World Wide Web.

CFV (Call For Votes)   The initiation of the voting period for a Usenet newsgroup. At least one (occasionally two or more) email address is customarily included as a repository for the votes.

channel   The name for a talk "room" under IRC.

chat   An online talk session, often with more than one person.

client   The user of a network service; also used to describe a computer that relies upon another for some or all of its resources.

CMC   Computer-mediated communication.

CU-SeeMe   Video conferencing software allowing Internet users to share live video and audio, regardless of distance.

CyberSex Explicit intimate communications between two people over the Internet.

Cyberspace A term coined by William Gibson in his fantasy novel *Neuromancer* to describe the "world" of computers and the society that gathers around them.

datagram The basic unit of information passed across the Internet. It contains a source and destination address along with data. Large messages are broken down into a sequence of IP datagrams.

disassembling Converting a binary program into human-readable, machine-language code.

DNS (Domain Name System) The method used to convert Internet names to their corresponding Internet numbers.

domain A part of the naming hierarchy. Syntactically, a domain name consists of a sequence of names or other words separated by periods.

dotted quad A set of four numbers connected with periods that make up an Internet address; for example, `147.31.254.130`.

email The vernacular abbreviation for electronic mail.

email address The UUCP or domain-based address for a user. For example, Janis Joplin's UUCP address might be `benz!janis`, while 'janis@porsche.-friend.org' could be her domain-based address.

e.News The fee-based Usenet newsfeed available from ClariNet Communications.

Ethernet A 10-million bit-per-second networking scheme originally developed by Xerox Corporation. Ethernet is widely used for LANs because it can network a wide variety of computers, it is not proprietary, and components are widely available from many commercial sources.

FDDI (Fiber Distributed Data Interface) An emerging standard for network technology, based on fiber optics, that has been established by ANSI. FDDI specifies a 100-million bit-per-second data rate. The access control mechanism uses token-ring technology.

flame Mail or a Usenet posting that is violently argumentative.

flamefest Massive flaming.

foo A place-holder for nearly anything—a variable, function, procedure, or even person. "A given user *foo* has the address foo@bar.com". The *New Hacker's Dictionary* has an excellent (one entire page) definition and historical background for foo.

FQDN (Fully Qualified Domain Name) The FQDN is the full site name of a system, rather than just its hostname. For example, the system `lisa` at Widener University has an FQDN of `lisa.cs.widener.edu`.

FTP (File Transfer Protocol) The Internet standard high-level protocol for transferring files from one computer to another.

FYI An abbreviation for the phrase "for your information." There is also a series of RFCs put out by the Network Information Center called FYIs; they address common questions of new users and many other useful things. See page 154 for instructions on retrieving FYIs.

gateway A special-purpose, dedicated computer that attaches to two or more networks and routes packets from one network to the other. In particular, an Internet gateway routes IP datagrams among the networks it connects. Gateways route packets to other gateways until they can be delivered to the final destination directly across one physical network.

GopherSpace The vast number of servers and areas of interest accessible through the Internet gopher.

GUI (Graphical User Interface) The aspects of a windowing system that make it unique; for example, the Motif GUI has a 3D feel to its buttons and menus.

header   The portion of a packet, preceding the actual data, containing source and destination addresses and error-checking fields. Also part of a message or news articlc.

hits   Matches found in a search; e.g., a veronica search for "NASA" will return a long list of hits for that query.

home page   A personal Web page.

hostname   The name given to a machine. (See also FQDN.)

hotlist   A person's selections of favorite Web pages.

image map   A graphic image on a Web page; you can click your mouse on a particular part of it to choose the next link you wish to visit.

IMHO (In My Humble Opinion)   This usually accompanies a statement that may bring about personal offense or strong disagreement.

internet   A collection of computers linked together by one or more networking protocols. An "internet" is not the same as "the Internet."

Internet   A concatenation of many individual TCP/IP campus, state, regional, and national networks (such as NSFnet, AARNet, and Milnet) into one single logical network sharing a common addressing scheme.

Internet number   The dotted-quad address used to specify a certain system. The Internet number for `cs.widener.edu` is `147.31.254.130`. A resolver is used to translate between host-names and Internet addresses.

interoperate The ability of multivendor computers to work together using a common set of protocols. With interoperability, PCs, Macs, Suns, etc., all work together allowing one host computer to communicate with and take advantage of the resources of another.

ISO (International Organization for Standardization) Coordinator of the main networking standards that are put into use today.

kernel The level of an operating system or networking system that contains the system-level commands or all the functions hidden from the user. In a Unix system, the kernel is a program that contains the device drivers, the memory management routines, the scheduler, and system calls. This program is always running while the system is operating.

LAN (Local Area Network) Any physical network technology that operates at high speed over short distances (up to a few thousand meters).

mail gateway A machine that connects to two or more electronic mail systems (especially dissimilar mail systems on two different networks) and transfers mail messages among them.

mailing list   A possibly moderated discussion group, distributed via email from a central computer maintaining the list of people involved in the discussion.

mail path   A series of machine names used to direct electronic mail from one user to another.

MBONE   The Internet multicast backbone (the MBONE). A "virtual network" that provides for Internet multicast packets to be routed across the Internet to a number of sites.

medium   The material used to support the transmission of data. This can be copper wire, coaxial cable, optical fiber, or electromagnetic wave (as in microwave).

multicast   Intended to be received by a number of hosts, as a multicast packet.

multiplex   The division of a single transmission medium into multiple logical channels supporting many simultaneous sessions. For example, one network may have simultaneous FTP, telnet, rlogin, and SMTP connections, all going at the same time.

net.citizen   An inhabitant of Cyberspace. One usually tries to be a good net.citizen, lest one be flamed.

netiquette   A pun on "etiquette"; proper behavior on the Net. See page 48.

network   A group of machines connected together so

they can transmit information to one another. There are two kinds of networks: local networks and remote networks.

newsgroup   A collection of messages on a particular topic, distributed via Usenet news.

NFS (Network File System)   A method developed by Sun Microsystems to allow computers to share files across a network in a way that makes them appear as if they're "local" to the system.

NIC   Network Information Center.

nickname   The name attached to a message displayed in IRC.

nixpub   A list maintained by Phil Eschallier (`phil@ls.com`) since 1987, detailing information on public-access Unix systems. Two versions, a long one providing all information and a short one listing the vital statistics of each site, are available from `listserv@bts.com`; put '`get pub nixpub.long`' or '`get pub nixpub.short`' in the body of your message.

NNTP (Network News Transfer Protocol)   The standard for Internet exchange of Usenet messages, published in RFC-977, *Network News Transfer Protocol: A Proposed Standard for the Stream-Based Transmission of News.*

node   A computer that is attached to a network; also called a host.

NSFnet The national backbone network, funded by the National Science Foundation and operated by the Merit Corporation, used to interconncct regional (mid-level) networks, such as WestNet, to one another.

NTP (Network Time Protocol) A protocol developed to maintain a common sense of "time" among Internet hosts around the world. Many systems on the Internet run NTP and have the same time (relative to Greenwich Mean Time), with a maximum difference of about one second.

operator The person running an IRC channel.

packet The unit of data sent across a packet-switching network. The term is used loosely. While some Internet literature uses it to refer specifically to data sent across a physical network, other literature views the Internet as a packet-switching network and describes IP datagrams as packets.

pass line A bet placed in the *pass line* of a craps table wins on the first roll of the dice yielding a 7 or 11 (termed a "natural") and loses if a 2, 3, or 12 comes up (called a "craps"). If none of these numbers appear, the value thrown becomes the "point," which must be rolled again before a 7 in order to win.

polling Connecting to another system to check for things like mail or news.

postmaster The person responsible for taking care of mail problems, answering queries about users and performing similar work for a given site.

protocols A formal description of message formats and the rules two computers must follow to exchange those messages. Protocols can describe low-level details of machine-to-machine interfaces (e.g., the order in which bits and bytes are sent across a wire) or high-level exchanges between allocation programs (e.g., the way in which two programs transfer a file across the Internet).

recursion The facility of a programming language to be able to call functions from within themselves.

resolve To translate an Internet name into its equivalent IP address or other DNS information.

RFD (Request For Discussion) Usually a two- to three-week period in which the particulars of newsgroup creation are battled out.

route The path that network traffic takes from its source to its destination.

router A dedicated computer (or other device) that sends packets from one place to another, paying attention to the current state of the network.

RTFM (Read The Fantastic Manual) This acronym is often used when someone asks a simple or common question. The word "Fantastic" is usually replaced with one much more vulgar.

server A computer that shares its resources, such as printers and files, with other computers on the network. An example of this is a Network File System (NFS) server, which shares its disk space with other computers.

signal-to-noise ratio When used in reference to Usenet activity, describes the relation between the amount of actual information in a discussion compared to quantity. More often than not, there's substantial activity in a newsgroup, but a very small number of those articles actually contain anything useful.

signature The small, usually four-line message at the bottom of a piece of email or Usenet article. In Unix, it's added by creating a file '.signature' in the user's home directory. Large signatures are a no-no.

smilies See `:-)`, page 213 .

SMTP (Simple Mail Transfer Protocol) The Internet standard protocol for transferring electronic mail messages from one computer to another. SMTP specifies how two mail systems interact and the format of control messages they exchange to transfer mail.

spam Blatant and high-volume Internet advertising, often performed by sending mail to hundreds of mailing lists simultaneously or posting an advertisement to thousands of newsgroups. The most aggressive approach to performing a *spam attack* is to meticulously make the posting to each group separately, thus making cancellation of the article difficult and time-consuming.

summarize To encapsulate a number of responses into one coherent, usable message. Often done on controlled mailing lists or active newsgroups to help reduce bandwidth.

synchronous Data communications in which transmissions are sent at a fixed rate, with the sending and receiving devices synchronized.

Tardis A device, once able to change shapes, that ended up frozen in the form of a British callbox in the Doctor Who television program. The term was coined by the character Susan Foreman in *Doctor Who and An Unearthly Child;* it stands for "Time And Relative Dimensions In Space."

TCP/IP (Transmission Control Protocol/Internet Protocol) A set of protocols, resulting from ARPA efforts, used by the Internet to support services such as remote login (telnet), file transfer (FTP), and mail (SMTP).

telnet The Internet standard protocol for remote terminal connection service. Telnet allows a

user at one site to interact with a remote
timesharing system at another site as if the
user's terminal were connected directly to the
remote computer.

terminal server A small, specialized, networked
computer that connects many terminals to a
LAN through one network connection. Any
user on the network can then connect to various network hosts.

TeX A free typesetting system by Donald Knuth.

TIA Thanks In Advance. Also, those who are very
clever sometimes use the interesting form
`aTdHvAaNnKcSe`.

twisted pair Cable made up of a pair of insulated
copper wires wrapped around each other to
cancel the effects of electrical noise.

URL Uniform Resource Locator. The identifier for
accessing a given World Wide Web page, FTP
site, etc.

UUCP (Unix-to-Unix Copy Program) A store-and-
forward system, primarily for Unix systems
but currently supported on other platforms
(e.g., VMS and personal computers).

virus A program that "infects" other programs by
embedding a copy of itself in them. (NHD)

WAN (Wide-Area Network) A network spanning
hundreds or thousands of miles.

WWW (World Wide Web) The interface used to present graphics, information, tables, and forms in a user-friendly setting.

worm Λ computer program that replicates itself. The Internet worm (see page 119) was perhaps the most famous; it successfully (and accidentally) duplicated itself on many of the systems across the Internet.

wrt With respect to.

veronica A tool to search GopherSpace; also an acronym for "Very Easy Rodent-Oriented Net-wide Index to Computerized Archives."

Zen A Japanese sect of Buddhism that stresses attaining enlightenment through intuition rather than by studying scripture.

"I hate definitions."
— Benjamin Disraeli, *Vivian Grey,*
bk i, chap ii

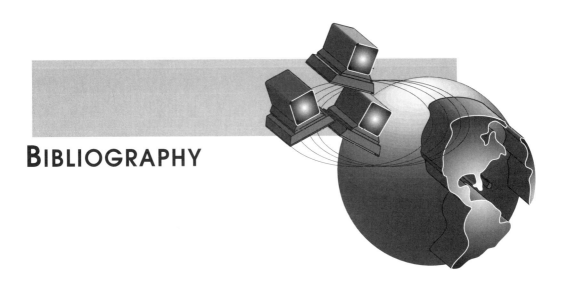

BIBLIOGRAPHY

What follows is a compendium of sources with information that will be of use to anyone reading this guide. Some of them were used in the writing of the book, while others are simply noted because they are a must for any good net.citizen's bookshelf.

Books

Baran, Nicholas (1995). *Inside the Information Superhighway*. The Coriolis Group: Scottsdale, Ariz.

Brunner, John (1975). *The Shockwave Rider*. Harper & Row: New York.

Comer, Douglas E. (1991). *Internetworking With TCP/IP*, 3 vols. Prentice Hall: Englewood Cliffs, N.J.

Davidson, John (1988). *An Introduction to TCP/IP*. Springer-Verlag: Berlin.

Dern, Daniel P. (1994). *The Internet Guide for New Users*. McGraw-Hill: New York.

Estrada, Susan (1993). *Connecting to the Internet.* O'Reilly and Associates: Sebastopol, Calif.

Fisher, Sharon (1993). *Riding the Internet Highway.* New Riders Publishing: Carmel, Ind.

Frey, Donnalyn, and Rick Adams (1994). *!@%:: A Directory of Electronic Mail Addressing and Networks.* O'Reilly and Associates: Sebastopol, Calif.

Gibbs, Mark, and Richard Smith (1995). *Navigating the Internet.* Sams Publishing: Carmel, Ind.

Gibson, William (1984). *Neuromancer.* Ace: New York.

Gilster, Paul (1994). *Finding It on the Internet.* John Wiley & Sons: New York.

Godin, Seth (1994). *E-Mail Addresses of the Rich & Famous.* Addison-Wesley: Reading, Mass.

Hafner, Katie, and John Markoff (1991). *Cyberpunk: Outlaws and Hackers on the Computer Frontier.* Simon & Schuster: New York.

Herrigel, Eugene (1953). *Zen in the Art of Archery.* Vintage Books: New York.

Hiltz, Starr Roxanne, and Murray Turoff (1993). *The Network Nation: Human Communication via Computer, Revised Edition.* MIT Press: Cambridge, Mass.

Krol, Ed (1992). *The Whole Internet User's Guide and Catalog.* O'Reilly and Associates: Sebastopol, Calif.

MKS Inc. (1995). *Internet Anywhere.* Prentice Hall: Englewood Cliffs, N.J.

Parker, Tracy LaQuey, and Jeanne C. Ryer (1994). *The Internet Companion: A Beginner's Guide to Global Networking.* Addison-Wesley: Reading, Mass.

LaQuey, Tracy (1990). *Users' Directory of Computer Networks.* Digital Press. Bedford, Mass.

Levy, Stephen (1984). *Hackers: Heroes of the Computer Revolution.* Anchor Press/Doubleday: Garden City, N.Y.

Lynch, Daniel, and Marshall Rose, eds. (1993). *Internet System Handbook.* Addison-Wesley: Reading, Mass.

Malamud, Carl (1992). *Exploring the Internet: A Technical Travelogue.* Prentice Hall: Englewood Cliffs, N.J.

Marine, April, et al. (1994). *Internet: Getting Started.* SRI International: Menlo Park, Calif.

Partridge, Craig (1988). *Innovations in Internetworking.* ARTECH House: Norwood, Mass.

Pirsig, Robert M. (1974). *Zen and the Art of Motorcycle Maintenance: An Inquiry into Values.* Morrow: New York.

Quarterman, John S. (1990). *The Matrix: Computer Networks and Conferencing Systems Worldwide.* Digital Press: Bedford, Mass.

Raymond, Eric, ed. (1994). *The New Hacker's Dictionary.* MIT Press: Cambridge, Mass.

Rheingold, Howard (1993). *The Virtual Community.* Harper Perennial: New York.

Rose, Donald (1994). *Minding Your Cyber-Manners on the Internet.* Alpha Books: Indianapolis.

Stoll, Clifford (1989). *The Cuckoo's Egg.* Doubleday: New York.

_____ (1995). *Silicon Snake Oil.* Doubleday: New York.

Tamosaitis, Nancy (1994). *net.talk*. Ziff-Davis Press: Emeryville, Calif.

_____ (1995). *net.sex*. Ziff-Davis Press: Emeryville, Calif.

Tanenbaum, Andrew S. (1988). *Computer Networks,* 2d ed. Prentice Hall: Englewood Cliffs, N.J.

Templeton, Brad (1995). *The Internet Joke Book*. Peer-to-Peer Communications: San Jose, Calif.

Tennant, Roy, John Ober, and Anne G. Lipow eds. (1993). *Crossing the Internet Threshold: An Instructional Handbook*. Library Solutions Press: Berkeley, Calif.

Todino, Grace (1986). *Using UUCP and USENET: A Nutshell Handbook*. O'Reilly and Associates: Newton, Mass.

The Waite Group (1991). *Unix Communications,* 2d ed. Howard W. Sams & Company: Indianapolis.

Wolf, Gary, and Michael Stein (1995). *Aether Madness*. Peachpit Press: Berkeley, Calif.

Periodicals, Papers, and Tapes

Arms, C. Using the National Networks: BITNET and the Internet. *Online* 14: 24-29.

Bailey, C.W. Electronic Publishing in Action: The Public Access Computer Systems Review and Other Electronic Serials. *Online* 15: 28-35.

Barlow, J. Coming Into The Country. *Communications of the ACM* (March 1991) 34:3:
Addresses "Cyberspace"—John Barlow was a co-founder of the EFF.

Bates, R., and White, K. *The KGB, the Computer, and Me.* Boston: WGBH for Nova, 1990. (58 min.)
This documentary was based on *The Cuckoo's Egg.*

Business Week (May 18, 1994).
Special issue on the Information Revolution.

Catlett, C.E. The NSFNET: Beginnings of a National Research Internet. *Academic Computing* 3: 19-21, 59-64.

Cisler, S. NREN Update: More Meetings and New Tools. *Database* (April 1991): 96-98.

Collyer, G., and H. Spencer. News Need Not Be Slow. *Proceedings of the 1987 Winter USENIX Conference:* 181-90. USENIX Association, Berkeley, Calif. (January 1987).

Coursey, D. Riding the Internet: The Mystery of This Vast Collection of Networks. *Infoworld* (February 4, 1991).

Denning, P. The Internet Worm. *American Scientist* (March-April 1989): 126-128.

____.The Science of Computing: Computer Networks. *American Scientist* (March-April 1985): 127-129.

de Llosa, Patty. Boom Time on the New Frontier. *Fortune* (Autumn 1993): 153-164.

de Vries, Peter J. L., and Karl Auerbach. Guide to Selecting an Internet Provider. *Network Computing* (May 15, 1995): 120.

Emtage, A., and P. Deutsch. archie—An Electronic Directory Service for the Internet. *Proceedings of the 1992 Winter USENIX Conference*: 93-110. USENIX Association, Berkeley, Calif. (January 1992).

Fisher, S. Whither NREN? *Byte* (July 1991): 181-190.

Franklin, Curtis Jr. A Glossary of Internet Terms. *Var Business* (September 1, 1994): 70.

Frey, D., and R. Adams. USENET: Death by Success? *UNIX REVIEW* (August 1987): 55-60.

Gartner, John, et al. Internet Software: Gateways to the World. *Windows Magazine* (May 1, 1995): 276.

Ginsberg, K. Getting from Here to There. *UNIX REVIEW* (January 1986): 45.

Higgins, Kelly Jackson. Commerce on the Net: What's the Holdup? *Open Systems Today* (October 31, 1994): 162.

Hiltz, S. R. The Human Element in Computerized Conferencing Systems. *Computer Networks* (December 1978): 421-428.

Horton, M. What is a Domain? *Proceedings of the Summer 1984 USENIX Conference:* 368-372. USENIX Association, Berkeley, Calif. (June 1984).

Hudgins-Bonafield, Christine. How Will the Internet Grow? *Network Computing* (March 1, 1995): 80.

Jacobsen, Ole J. Information on TCP/IP. *ConneXions— The Interoperability Report* (July 1988): 14-15.

Jennings, D., et al. Computer Networking for Scientists. *Science* (February 28, 1986): 943-950.

Jones, P. *What is the Internet?* Available on `ftp.oit.unc.edu` in 'pub/docs/whatis.internet'.

Krol, E. *The Hitchhiker's Guide to the Internet.* RFC-1118.

Lynch, C., and C. Preston. INTERNET access to information resources. *Annual Review of Information Sci-*

ence and Technology (ARIST—American Society for Information Science) 25: 263-311.

Markoff, J. "Author of computer 'virus' is son of U.S. electronic security expert." *New York Times* (Nov. 5, 1988): A1. Purists will notice the misuse of the term *virus*, rather than *worm*, in the title of the article.

_____."Computer snarl: A 'back door' ajar." *New York Times* (Nov. 7, 1988): B10.

Martin, J. *There's Gold in Them Thar Networks! or Searching for Treasure in All the Wrong Places.* FYI-10 and RFC-1290.

McQuillan, J. M., and Walden, D. C. The ARPA Network Design Decisions. *Computer Networks* (1977): 243-289.

Messmer, E. Internet Retrieval Tools Go On Market. *Network World* (Feb. 15, 1993): 29.

Ornstein, S. M. A letter concerning the Internet worm. *Communications of the ACM* (June 1989) 32:6.

Partridge, C. Mail Routing Using Domain Names: An Informal Tour. *Proceedings of the 1986 Summer USENIX Conference:* 366-76. USENIX Association, Berkeley, Calif. (June 1986).

Pethia, R., and K. van Wyk. *Computer Emergency Response—An International Problem.* Available on `cert.sei.cmu.edu` in '`/pub/doc`'. Paper describing CERT and its origins.

Polly, J. A. *Surfing the INTERNET: An Introduction.* Available on `nysernet.org` in the directory '`pub/resources/guides`'. Excellent and entertaining guide to the Net.

Quarterman, J. Etiquette and Ethics. *ConneXions—The Interoperability Report* (March 1989): 12-16.

____.Internet Misconceptions. *ComputerWorld* (Feb 22, 1993): 83.

____.Notable Computer Networks. *Communications of the ACM* 29:10 (October 1986).
This was the predecessor to *The Matrix*.

Scientific American **265**:3 (September 1991). This issue was dedicated to "Communications, Computers and Networks"; it contains articles addressing the past, present, and future of computer networking.

Seeley, D. A tour of the worm. *Proceedings of the 1989 Winter USENIX Conference:* 287-304. USENIX Association, Berkeley, Calif. (February 1989).

Shapiro, N., and R. Anderson. *Toward an Ethics and Etiquette for Electronic Mail*. Santa Monica, Calif.: RAND Corporation, Report R-3283-NSF/RC. Available on `rand.org` in '`pub/Reports`'.

Shulman, G. Legal Research on USENET Liability Issues. *;login: The USENIX Association Newsletter* (December 1984): 11-17.

Smith, K. E-Mail to Anywhere. *PC World* (March 1988): 220-223.

Spafford, Eugene H. The Internet Worm: Crisis and Aftermath. *Communications of the ACM* 32:6 (June 1989): 678-687.

Stanton, D. *AARNet and the Academic Library: A Report on the Seminar/Workshop Held February 1992*. Murdoch, W.A.: Murdoch University Library. Available via anonymous FTP from `csuvax1.csu.murdoch.edu.au` in '`pub/library`' as '`newcwkshp.rpt`'.

Stoll, C. Stalking the Wily Hacker. *Communications of the ACM* 31:5 (May 1988): 484-497.
This article grew into the book *The Cuckoo's Egg.*

U.S. Gen'l. Accounting Ofc. Computer Security: Virus Highlights Need for Improved Internet Management. *GAO/ IMTEC* -89 -57, (1989).
Addresses the Internet worm .

Wright, Robert. Voice of America: Overhearing the Internet. *The New Republic* (September 13, 1993): 20-27.

"All the rest is mere fine writing."
— Paul Verlaine, *Art poetique,* 1882.

INDEX

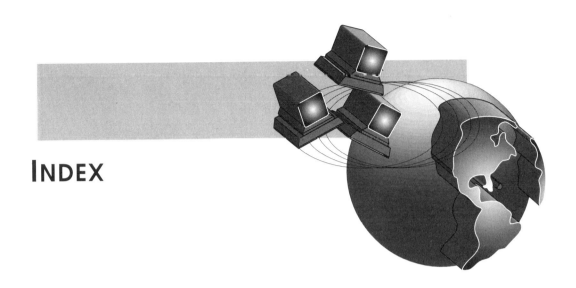

B

I

O